BLOCKCHAIN

Exploring the Potential of Blockchain:

Revolutionizing Industries and Beyond

Jasper Donovan

TABLE OF CONTENTS

INTRODUCTION

Welcome to "Blockchain: Exploring the Potential of Blockchain - Revolutionizing Industries and Beyond." The intriguing world of blockchain technology and its disruptive effects on numerous industries and society as a whole are explored in this e-book.

Blockchain has emerged as a ground-breaking technology that is disrupting established structures and creating novel opportunities across sectors. Innovative applications have emerged as a result of its decentralized structure, immutability, and transparency, and they have the potential to alter the way we connect fundamentally, transact commerce, and govern.

In this thorough guide, we'll delve into the underlying ideas behind blockchain, reveal how it operates, and examine the plethora of uses it may be put to. The potential of blockchain is limitless and spans a broader range of industries, including finance, supply chain management, healthcare, government services, energy, sustainability, and even social and humanitarian sectors.

We will see how blockchain transforms the financial landscape, revolutionizes supply chain management, protects sensitive healthcare data, empowers governments, and supports sustainability initiatives through an exhaustive study of real-world application cases. We will also look at the difficulties and restrictions that come with implementing blockchain technology and the new tendencies and innovations influencing its course in the future.

We'll also look outside of industries to see how blockchain affects society and the world. Blockchain is paving the way for positive change and inclusivity, especially in underserved communities, in everything from philanthropy to voting systems, refugee aid to economic empowerment.

This e-book will provide you a thorough grasp of this revolutionary technology and its implications, whether you are a technology enthusiast, an entrepreneur looking for creative solutions, a professional in a certain area, or simply interested in the possibilities of blockchain.

Join us as we explore the complex world of blockchain, explore its potential, and get a taste of the fascinating future it promises. Let's explore blockchain's potential and its amazing journey to revolutionize industries and more.

CHAPTER I

Understanding the Inner Workings of Blockchain

Exploring blockchain components: blocks, transactions, and nodes

Due to its capacity to transform industries and improve security and transparency in numerous processes, blockchain technology has attracted a lot of attention and recognition in recent years. Blocks, transactions, and nodes are at the core of blockchain technology. To fully comprehend the inner workings of blockchain and its disruptive potential, it is essential to comprehend these fundamental components. We will delve into each of these elements in-depth in this section, highlighting their significance and outlining how they support the reliability and integrity of blockchain networks.

The core of the entire system, and the basis for blockchain technology, are blocks. A block is a type of data container that keeps a group of transactions and other metadata together. Typically, a block's structure is made up of a header, transaction data, and metadata.

A blockchain network is made up of blocks, which act as data containers. A block's header contains essential information, such as a timestamp, a unique block identifier, and a reference to the previous block. Transaction data, on the other hand, contains the details of the transactions recorded within the block. Finally, metadata includes additional information, such as the nonce used in mining.

The process of block generation is often referred to as mining. Miners compete to solve difficult mathematical problems using computational power, and the first miner to find a solution adds a new block to the blockchain. This process is often associated with the proof-of-work (PoW) consensus algorithm. To ensure the integrity as well as security of the blockchain, each block is linked to the previous block through a unique identifier called a hash. Hash functions, such as SHA-256, are used to generate these identifiers. The hash of a block includes the block's data and the hash of the previous block, generating a chain of blocks that are cryptographically connected.

Once a block is generated, it needs to be validated and accepted by the network. Consensus algorithms play a crucial role in this process. Proof of Work (PoW) is one widely used consensus algorithm, where miners solve computational puzzles to find a nonce that, when combined with the block data, produces a hash below a certain target value. This process requires significant computational power and ensures that blocks are added to the blockchain at a controlled rate. Other consensus algorithms, like the Proof of Stake (PoS), determine block validators based on their stake in the network. Validators are chosen to create new blocks, and their probability of being selected is proportional to the number of tokens they hold. This approach aims to reduce energy consumption associated with PoW.

The size of a block plays a crucial role in the scalability and efficiency of a blockchain network. Larger blocks can accommodate more transactions, but they also require more storage and increase the time required for propagation. The block size limitation presents a challenge for blockchain scalability. In response to this challenge, various approaches have been proposed to optimize block size and improve scalability. Segregated Witness (SegWit) is one such solution that separates transaction data from signature data, allowing more transactions to be included in a block without increasing its size. Additionally, the Lightning Network and other layer-two solutions aim to enable off-chain transactions, further enhancing scalability.

Transactions are the lifeblood of a blockchain network. They represent the transfer of value, ownership, or information between participants. Understanding the structure and characteristics of transactions is vital to grasp how blockchain achieves trust and transparency.

In a blockchain network, transactions are structured sets of data that include inputs, outputs, and scripts. Inputs refer to the sources of funds for a transaction, typically referencing unspent transaction outputs (UTXOs) from previous transactions. Outputs represent the destinations of the funds being transferred, specifying the recipient addresses and the corresponding amounts. To ensure the security as well as the integrity of transactions, blockchain employs cryptographic techniques such as digital signatures. Digital signatures are created using the private key of the sender and can be verified using the corresponding public key. This process ensures that only the rightful owner of a private key can initiate transactions.

Before a transaction is added to a block, it undergoes a verification process to guarantee its validity. In a blockchain network, this verification is performed by nodes that validate the transaction against specific rules defined by the consensus algorithm. For example, in a Bitcoin network, nodes verify that the inputs of a transaction are legitimate UTXOs and that the digital signatures are valid. If a transaction fails to meet these criteria, it is considered invalid and will not be included in a block.

Blockchain technology inherently offers transparency since every transaction is recorded on the blockchain and it is accessible to all participants. However, privacy and anonymity are also important considerations.

Public and private key cryptography plays a crucial role in ensuring privacy in blockchain transactions. Public keys are used to generate addresses that can receive funds, while private keys are kept secret and used to sign transactions. While transactions are recorded publicly, the identities of the participants are not necessarily revealed. Instead, participants are pseudonymous, as they are identified by their public keys or addresses. To enhance privacy, various techniques have been developed, such as zero-knowledge proofs and ring signatures. Zero-knowledge proofs allow a party to prove knowledge of certain information without revealing the real information. Ring signatures, on the other hand, enable a signer to blend their signature with a group of other signatures, making it difficult to determine the actual signer.

Nodes are the participants that form the decentralized network of a blockchain. They play a vital role in maintaining the integrity, security, and consensus of the network. Nodes can be classified into different roles, including full nodes, light nodes, and mining nodes. The blockchain is entirely stored on full nodes, which also take part in relaying and validating transactions and blocks. Light nodes, also known as lightweight or SPV (Simple Payment Verification) nodes, store only a fraction of the blockchain data and rely on full nodes for transaction verification. Mining nodes are specialized nodes that contribute computational power to the mining process and add new blocks to the blockchain.

Nodes communicate with one another using a peer-to-peer network architecture, where each node maintains connections with multiple other nodes. This network structure ensures the decentralized and distributed nature of blockchain. Transactions and blocks are propagated through the network using various network protocols, such as gossip, flooding, and broadcasting. Gossip protocols disseminate information to a subset of nodes, which then relay it further, creating an efficient information dissemination process. Flooding protocols, on the other hand, propagate information to all connected nodes, ensuring that the information reaches every corner of the network.

Nodes are incentivized to participate in blockchain networks through various mechanisms. In proof-of-work (PoW) systems like Bitcoin, mining nodes are rewarded with newly generated cryptocurrency and transaction fees for their computational efforts in solving complex puzzles. This incentivizes miners to compete and contribute their computational power to secure the network. In proof-of-stake (PoS) systems, nodes are chosen as validators based on the number of tokens they hold. Validators are incentivized through rewards generated by transaction fees. The PoS consensus algorithm reduces energy consumption compared to PoW systems but requires a high level of stakeholder participation.

Nodes in a blockchain network need to remain synchronized to maintain consensus. When a new block is added to the blockchain, nodes update their local copies to reflect the latest state of the network. However, conflicts can arise when multiple nodes find solutions to the mining problem simultaneously, leading to multiple valid blocks being added to the blockchain at the same time. This results in a fork in the chain, where the network temporarily diverges into multiple branches. To resolve forks and maintain a single version of the truth, consensus rules are followed. The longest chain rule is one such rule, where nodes accept the longest chain as the valid one. This ensures that the network eventually converges to a single chain, with the forked blocks being discarded.

Proof of Work, Proof of Stake, and other consensus mechanisms

Blockchain technology relies heavily on consensus mechanisms to maintain consistency and agreement among users of a decentralized network. The two well-known consensus algorithms used in blockchain systems are Proof of Work (PoW) and Proof of Stake (PoS). We will explore these two consensus methods in depth in this section, as well as other recently developed consensus algorithms. Understanding these methods, as well as their advantages and disadvantages, will help us better understand the crucial elements that influence the security, scalability, and energy efficiency of blockchain networks.

The ground-breaking consensus method that supports Bitcoin and many other blockchain networks is called Proof of Work. In order to add new blocks to the blockchain, participants in PoW—known as miners—must use computational work to solve difficult mathematical puzzles.

The mining process in PoW involves miners competing to solve a computationally intensive mathematical puzzle. This process demands significant computational power and energy consumption. Miners utilize their computing resources to find a nonce value that, when combined with the block data, produces a hash value below a predetermined target value. New cryptocurrency and transaction fees are awarded to the miner who completes the puzzle successfully.

One of the primary advantages of PoW is its robustness against attacks. The computational puzzle required to mine a block makes it economically infeasible for an attacker to control a majority of the network's computing power, mitigating the risk of Sybil attacks. The consensus is achieved by the majority of miners honestly contributing their computational resources to secure the network, ensuring the integrity of the blockchain.

While PoW has proven its security, it faces challenges in scalability and energy consumption. As the network grows, the computational power needed for mining increases, resulting in longer block validation times and higher transaction fees. Additionally, the energy consumption associated with PoW has raised environmental concerns. To address scalability, various approaches have been proposed, including the increased of block size, implementing off-chain scaling solutions like the Lightning Network, or utilizing layer-two protocols. Additionally, efforts are being made to improve energy efficiency by exploring alternative consensus mechanisms or integrating renewable energy sources into the mining process.

Proof of Stake (PoS) emerged as an alternative to PoW, addressing some of its scalability and energy consumption challenges by redefining the consensus process. PoS determines block validators based on the number of cryptocurrency tokens they hold, rather than computational power.

In PoS, validators are chosen to create new blocks based on their stake or ownership of the cryptocurrency. The more tokens a validator holds, the higher the chances of being selected to validate and add a new block. This approach eliminates the need for resource-intensive mining and significantly reduces energy consumption.

While PoS offers scalability and energy efficiency advantages, there are concerns regarding the security of the network. To address these concerns, PoS incorporates economic incentives and penalties. Validators are required to lock up a certain number of tokens as a security deposit, known as a stake. Validators who behave dishonestly or attempt to attack the network may have their stakes slashed, resulting in financial loss. This economic disincentive ensures that validators act in the best interest of the network.

In addition to traditional PoS, several variations and hybrid models have been developed to enhance the consensus mechanism. Delegated Proof of Stake (DPoS) introduces a delegate system where a limited number of trusted nodes are elected to validate transactions and create blocks. This approach improves scalability and transaction throughput, but it may raise concerns about centralization.

Hybrid consensus mechanisms combine PoW and PoS to harness the benefits of both. By utilizing PoW for block validation and PoS for selecting block validators, these hybrid models aim to achieve a balance between security, decentralization, and scalability.

While PoW and PoS dominate the blockchain landscape, several alternative and emerging consensus mechanisms are being explored, each with its unique characteristics and advantages.

Delegated Proof of Stake (DPoS) introduces a system where participants elect a limited number of trusted nodes to validate transactions and create blocks. These nodes, known as delegates, take turns producing blocks on behalf of the network. This approach improves scalability and transaction throughput by reducing the number of validators and enabling faster block confirmation times. However, DPoS can raise concerns about centralization, as the election process may favor larger stakeholders or certain entities. Nevertheless, it offers practical solutions for blockchain networks that require high throughput and quick transaction finality.

Practical Byzantine Fault Tolerance (PBFT) is a consensus mechanism that focuses on achieving consensus in Byzantine fault-prone environments, where participants may exhibit malicious behavior or fail arbitrarily. It utilizes a consensus algorithm that allows a group of nodes, known as replicas, to agree on the order of transactions through a series of message exchanges. PBFT offers fast transaction finality and high throughput compared to PoW and PoS. However, it typically requires a fixed set of known and trusted nodes, limiting its applicability in public and permissionless blockchain networks.

Proof of Authority (PoA) is a consensus mechanism that relies on trusted validators or authorities to create new blocks and validate transactions. Validators are identified by their reputation, identity, or endorsement from reputable organizations. PoA offers fast block confirmation times, low energy consumption, and resistance to Sybil attacks. However, PoA sacrifices decentralization as it relies on a limited number of trusted validators. It is typically used in private and consortium blockchain networks where trust among participants is already established.

Directed Acyclic Graph (DAG) and Hashgraph are alternative data structures and consensus mechanisms that aim to overcome the scalability limitations of traditional blockchain systems. DAG-based networks, such as IOTA's Tangle, utilize a graph structure where each transaction verifies and references previous transactions. This allows for parallel processing of transactions, resulting in high scalability and fast confirmation times. Similarly, Hashgraph utilizes a gossip protocol and voting-based consensus algorithm to achieve consensus in a highly efficient manner.

Choosing an appropriate consensus mechanism depends on various factors, including the specific goals, requirements, and characteristics of the blockchain network.

Different consensus mechanisms offer varying levels of security and trust assumptions. Evaluating the security model of a consensus mechanism involves assessing its resistance to attacks, the cost of attacking the network, and the trustworthiness of participants. The level of decentralization and the consensus algorithm's resilience to various types of attacks, such as 51% attacks or collusion attacks, should be considered.

Scalability is a critical consideration for blockchain networks, especially as transaction volumes increase. The consensus mechanism should be able to handle a growing number of transactions without compromising performance. Factors to consider include block size, block confirmation times, network latency, and the ability to scale horizontally or vertically.

Energy consumption has become a significant concern associated with PoW-based blockchain networks. Selecting a consensus mechanism that reduces energy consumption or utilizes renewable energy sources can mitigate environmental impacts. PoS and other energy-efficient mechanisms offer alternatives that aim to reduce energy consumption without compromising security.

Consensus mechanisms may also influence the governance and decision-making process within a blockchain network. Some mechanisms may provide more democratic or decentralized governance structures, where participants have a say in protocol upgrades or decision-making processes. Understanding the governance implications and ensuring alignment with the network's objectives and values is crucial when selecting a consensus mechanism.

The blockchain ecosystem continues to evolve rapidly, and several ongoing research efforts aim to address the limitations and improve the efficiency of existing consensus mechanisms.

Researchers are actively working on improving PoS-based consensus mechanisms. Efforts include developing solutions to mitigate the "Nothing at Stake" problem, exploring reputation-based mechanisms, and integrating performance metrics to ensure the network's security and integrity.

Practical Byzantine Fault Tolerance (PBFT) and its variants continue to be a subject of research for consensus mechanisms beyond PoW and PoS. Further exploration and development of these mechanisms can lead to more efficient and secure consensus algorithms suitable for different types of blockchain networks.

Scalability remains a crucial challenge for blockchain technology. Ongoing research focuses on developing innovative solutions such as layer-two protocols (e.g., Lightning Network), sharding, and partitioning techniques to enable higher transaction throughput and improve network scalability.

Addressing the energy consumption concerns associated with PoW-based networks is a priority in the blockchain community. Ongoing efforts aim to develop consensus mechanisms that reduce energy consumption, integrate renewable energy sources, or explore alternative approaches to achieve consensus while maintaining security and decentralization.

Cryptography in blockchain: public and private keys, digital signatures

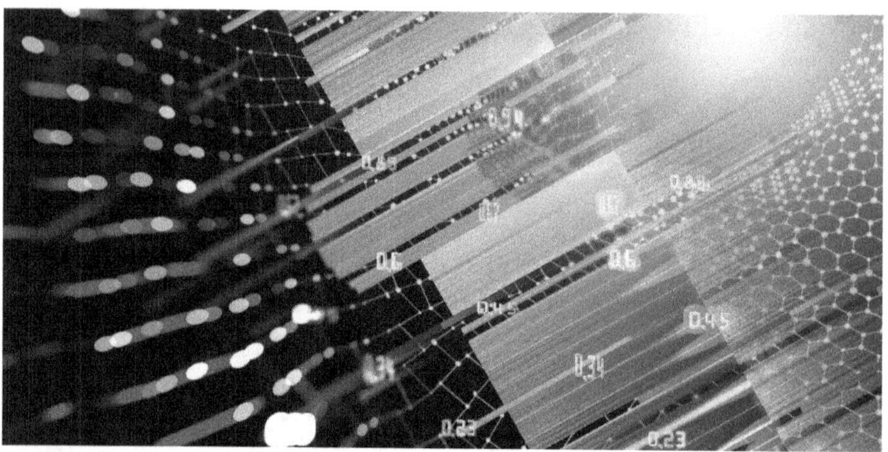

A key component of blockchain technology, cryptography ensures the security, privacy, and integrity of decentralized networks. Digital signatures, public and private keys, and the cryptographic framework of blockchain are at the foundation of the technology. We will examine the foundational ideas of cryptography in blockchain in this section, highlighting the functions of public and private keys as well as the significance of digital signatures. We can comprehend how blockchain delivers secure transactions, data integrity, and participant identification by comprehending these cryptographic components.

Asymmetric cryptography, commonly referred to as public and private cryptography, is the cornerstone of safe communication in blockchain networks. A pair of mathematically related keys—a public key and a corresponding private key—are used in this cryptographic technique.

The process of generating public and private keys involves complex mathematical algorithms. A user's private key is generated randomly and kept secret, while the corresponding public key is derived from the private key using mathematical operations. The public key is then shared with other participants in the network. In blockchain, participants use their private keys to create digital signatures and decrypt encrypted data. The private key should be securely stored and kept confidential to prevent unauthorized access and ensure the security of blockchain transactions.

Public keys are used for encryption, allowing anyone to encrypt data intended for a specific participant. However, only the corresponding private key holder can decrypt the encrypted data. This ensures confidentiality and privacy in blockchain transactions and communications. When a participant wants to send a secure message or initiate a transaction, they encrypt the data using the recipient's public key. Only the recipient, who have the corresponding private key, can decrypt the message or transaction data and access the original content.

Private keys play a crucial role in generating digital signatures, which serve as a means of authentication and integrity verification. By digitally signing a message or transaction, a participant provides proof of authenticity and ensures that the content has not been tampered with. To create a digital signature, the sender uses their private key to perform a cryptographic operation on the message or transaction data. This operation produces a unique digital signature that is specific to the content being signed and the private key used. The virtual signature is then attached to the message or transaction, allowing recipients to verify the authenticity and integrity of the content.

Recipients can verify the digital signature using the sender's public key. By applying a matching cryptographic operation to the received content and comparing it to the digital signature, the recipient can confirm whether the content has been tampered with or altered. This process ensures the integrity of blockchain transactions and prevents unauthorized modifications. Digital signatures provide non-repudiation, ensuring that the sender cannot deny their participation or the authenticity of a transaction. By associating the digital signature with the sender's private key, it becomes nearly impossible for the sender to repudiate their actions, providing a high level of trust and accountability in blockchain networks.

Secure hash functions are an essential cryptographic tool utilized in blockchain to safeguard the integrity of data, ensuring that it remains unchanged and tamper-proof.

A mathematical process known as a hash function transforms input (data or message) of any size into a fixed-length string of characters. Since it is intended to be a one-way function, it would be computationally impossible to reconstruct the original input from the hash value. In blockchain, secure hash functions are used to create a unique hash value for each block in the chain. This hash value is derived by including the block's data, previous block's hash, and other relevant information. By including the previous block's hash, any alteration to a block's data would result in a different hash value, immediately signaling tampering or data manipulation.

The use of secure hash functions ensures the integrity and immutability of blockchain data. Once a block is added to the blockchain, its hash value becomes a crucial component of subsequent blocks. Any change to the data within a block would lead to a different hash value, disrupting the chain of blocks and alerting participants to potential tampering. Secure hash functions provide a mechanism to verify the integrity of blockchain data without revealing the original content. Participants can independently compute the hash value of a block and compare it to the stored hash value. If the two values match, it indicates that the data remains intact and unaltered.

Merkle trees, also known as hash trees, are data structures that allow for efficient and secure verification of data integrity. In blockchain, Merkle trees are constructed by recursively hashing the transaction data until a single root hash, known as the Merkle root, is obtained. By incorporating the Merkle root in the block header, participants can efficiently verify the integrity of specific transactions within a block. Merkle trees enable efficient verification by reducing the amount of data that needs to be processed. Instead of verifying each transaction individually, participants only need to verify the Merkle root, which represents the collective integrity of all transactions within a block. This approach enhances the scalability of blockchain networks by minimizing computational overhead while ensuring data integrity.

Proper key management is crucial in blockchain to ensure the security and confidentiality of participant identities and transactions.

Additionally, key management practices mitigate the risks of key loss, theft, or unauthorized access.

Private keys must be securely stored to avoid unauthorized access or theft. Storing private keys on secure hardware devices, known as hardware wallets, provides an added layer of protection. Hardware wallets ensure that private keys are stored offline and inaccessible to potential attackers. In cases where hardware wallets are not feasible, private keys can be stored in encrypted digital containers protected by strong passwords. This approach ensures that even if the container is compromised, the private keys remain encrypted and inaccessible without the correct password.

Generating strong and random private keys is paramount to ensure the security of blockchain participants. Random number generators and cryptographic libraries are used to generate private keys with a sufficiently high level of entropy. Additionally, key rotation practices, where new key pairs are generated periodically, enhance security by limiting the potential impact of key compromise. Regularly rotating private keys reduces the window of opportunity for attackers and enhances the overall security of blockchain networks.

Multi-signature (multi-sig) addresses add an extra layer of security to blockchain transactions by requiring multiple private keys to authorize a transaction. This mechanism ensures that no single participant can unilaterally initiate a transaction, reducing the risk of fraudulent or unauthorized transactions. Multi-signature addresses involve multiple participants each having their own private key. To authorize a transaction, a specified number of participants must sign the transaction using their private keys. This approach adds redundancy and security to the transaction validation process, preventing unauthorized access and enhancing trust in blockchain networks.

The advent of quantum computing poses potential threats to the security of traditional cryptographic algorithms used in blockchain. Quantum computers have the potential to break commonly used cryptographic algorithms, rendering current cryptographic systems vulnerable.

Post-quantum cryptography research aims to develop algorithms that are resistant to attacks by quantum computers, ensuring the long-term security of blockchain systems. Researchers are actively exploring quantum-resistant algorithms, such as lattice-based cryptography, code-based cryptography, and multivariate cryptography, to address the challenges posed by quantum computing.

CHAPTER II

Blockchain Applications and Use Cases

Financial Sector Transformation

- **Cryptocurrencies and digital assets**

Blockchain technology was initially and foremost used in the development of cryptocurrencies. Cryptocurrencies allow for secure peer-to-peer transactions without the use of middlemen or centralized authority since they are digital currencies that run on decentralized networks.

At the heart of cryptocurrencies is the ability to facilitate decentralized payments and transactions. Blockchain technology, with its decentralized nature and distributed ledger, enables secure and transparent transactions directly between participants. Transactions are validated and recorded in a transparent manner, ensuring the integrity and immutability of the transaction history. Cryptocurrencies eliminate the need for traditional financial intermediaries, such as banks, by leveraging blockchain's consensus mechanisms and cryptographic techniques to validate and authenticate transactions. This decentralized approach offers greater control and autonomy to individuals, while reducing transaction fees and processing times.

One of the significant advantages of cryptocurrencies is their potential to foster financial inclusion. Blockchain technology allows individuals who are unbanked as well as underbanked to access financial services and participate in the global economy. With a smartphone and internet connectivity, anyone can create a cryptocurrency wallet and engage in peer-to-peer transactions. Moreover, cryptocurrencies enable efficient cross-border transactions. Traditional banking systems often impose high fees and lengthy settlement times for international transfers. Cryptocurrencies can significantly reduce these barriers by enabling fast, secure, and low-cost cross-border transactions, empowering individuals and businesses with greater financial accessibility.

Price volatility has been a major concern for cryptocurrencies, hindering their adoption for everyday transactions and store of value purposes. Stablecoins, a type of cryptocurrency, address this issue by maintaining a stable value. Stablecoins are pegged to an external asset, like a fiat currency or a commodity, providing price stability and minimizing volatility. Stablecoins offer the benefits of cryptocurrencies, such as fast and secure transactions, while mitigating the price volatility associated with other digital assets. They serve as a bridge between the world of cryptocurrencies and traditional financial systems, providing a stable and reliable digital medium of exchange.

Blockchain technology has paved the way for the tokenization of real-world assets, enabling fractional ownership, increased liquidity, and enhanced accessibility to traditionally illiquid assets.

Tokenization involves representing physical assets, such as real estate, art, or precious metals, as digital tokens on a blockchain. This process allows for the fractional ownership of these assets, breaking them into smaller, tradable units. Tokenization democratizes investment opportunities by providing access to assets that were traditionally reserved for high-net-worth individuals or institutional investors. By tokenizing assets, blockchain technology facilitates increased liquidity. Previously illiquid assets, such as real estate or fine art, can now be easily bought, sold, and traded on blockchain-based platforms, offering individuals and businesses new avenues for investment and diversification.

Security tokens are a type of token that represents ownership in traditional financial assets, such as stocks, bonds, or investment funds. These tokens leverage blockchain technology to enhance transparency, automate compliance, and enable programmable features through smart contracts. Security tokens adhere to existing regulatory frameworks, providing a secure and compliant way to tokenize traditional financial assets. They offer fractional ownership, efficient transferability, and simplified settlement processes, while ensuring transparency and compliance with securities regulations.

Non-Fungible Tokens (NFTs) are unique digital assets that can represent ownership of digital or physical items, such as artwork, music, or virtual real estate. NFTs utilize blockchain technology to establish provenance, authenticity, and scarcity, revolutionizing the world of digital collectibles. It enables artists, content creators, and collectors to tokenize and trade digital assets in a secure and transparent manner. Blockchain ensures the authenticity and ownership history of NFTs, providing a new business model for artists and content creators to monetize their work and engage directly with their audience.

Decentralized Finance, or DeFi, leverages blockchain technology to create an open and permissionless financial ecosystem that operates without intermediaries, enabling individuals to access financial services traditionally offered by banks and other financial institutions.

DeFi platforms facilitate peer-to-peer lending and borrowing, allowing individuals to lend or borrow digital assets directly from other participants in the network. Smart contracts automate the lending and repayment process, reducing the requirement for intermediaries and enhancing transparency. By eliminating the need for traditional lenders, DeFi lending platforms provide individuals with greater access to credit and financial services, particularly in regions where banking services are limited. Moreover, these platforms offer competitive interest rates and enable borrowers to leverage their digital assets as collateral.

Users can trade digital assets directly with one another without the use of centralized middlemen due to decentralized exchanges (DEXs). These platforms utilize smart contracts to enable trustless and transparent transactions, removing the need for intermediaries to hold custody of users' assets. It offers greater security, privacy, and control over assets compared to centralized exchanges. Users retain ownership of their assets throughout the trading process, reducing the risk of hacks, theft, or loss due to exchange vulnerabilities.

Yield farming and liquidity mining are popular practices in the DeFi ecosystem that incentivize participants to contribute liquidity to decentralized protocols. Users can lock their digital assets in liquidity pools and earn additional tokens as rewards. These mechanisms promote liquidity and participation in DeFi protocols while allowing individuals to earn passive income. By providing liquidity, users contribute to the general liquidity of the DeFi ecosystem, enabling efficient price discovery and trading.

Blockchain technology offers solutions for enhancing supply chain management, improving transparency, traceability, and trust in complex supply chains.

Blockchain-based supply chain solutions enable the tracking and verification of product authenticity throughout the supply chain. Each product can be assigned a special digital identifier, such as a QR code or an RFID tag, which is recorded on the blockchain. This enables consumers and stakeholders to verify the origin and authenticity of goods, reducing the risk of counterfeit products entering the market.

Blockchain ensures the integrity as well as immutability of the recorded information, making it nearly impossible to tamper with or manipulate product data. This transparency builds trust between consumers and producers, fosters brand reputation, and protects consumers from fraudulent or unsafe products.

Complex supply chains often suffer from inefficiencies, lack of transparency, and information asymmetry. Blockchain-based supply chain solutions address these challenges by providing a shared, tamper-resistant ledger that allows participants to track the movement of goods, verify certifications, and ensure compliance with regulations. By recording transactions, certifications, and other relevant information on the blockchain, supply chain participants can have real-time visibility into the status and also the location of goods. This transparency reduces delays, improves efficiency, and enables prompt resolution of any issues or disputes that may arise during the supply chain process.

Blockchain enables the tracking of supply chain attributes, such as fair trade practices, labor conditions, and environmental impact. By recording these attributes on the blockchain, companies can demonstrate ethical sourcing practices and sustainability initiatives, empowering consumers to make informed choices and support responsible business practices. Blockchain-based supply chain solutions enable consumers to verify the authenticity of eco-friendly certifications, fair trade labels, or organic production methods. This transparency encourages companies to adopt more sustainable and ethical practices, leading to positive social and environmental impacts.

Blockchain-based governance models and Decentralized Autonomous Organizations (DAOs) offer new approaches to decision-making, transparency, and community participation.

Blockchain enables decentralized governance models where participants can vote on proposals, protocol upgrades, and other decisions that impact the blockchain network or specific projects. Each participant's voting power is determined by the number of tokens they hold, fostering a more democratic and inclusive decision-making process. Decentralized governance allows participants to actively shape the direction and development of blockchain projects, creating a sense of ownership and community engagement. By decentralizing decision-making, blockchain networks aim to eliminate central points of control and foster greater transparency and fairness.

Decentralized Autonomous Organizations (DAOs) are blockchain-based organizations governed by smart contracts and community voting. These organizations operate without central authorities, enabling participants to collectively make decisions, allocate resources, and govern the organization's activities. DAOs utilize blockchain technology to facilitate transparent and auditable governance processes. Smart contracts execute predefined rules and distribute funds based on community voting outcomes. This eliminates the need for traditional hierarchical structures, allowing for more decentralized and community-driven decision-making.

- **Smart contracts and decentralized finance (DeFi)**

Blockchain technology has introduced the concept of smart contracts, which are self-executing digital contracts that operate on a blockchain. These contracts are programmable and automatically execute predefined actions when specific conditions are met. Smart contracts take away the need for intermediaries and ensure trust and transparency in digital agreements.

Smart contracts' capacity to facilitate trustless interactions is one of the primary benefits they offer. Trust is established through blockchain's immutability and transparency, which ensures that the terms and conditions of a smart contract cannot be altered without consensus from all involved parties. This eliminates the need for intermediaries, such as lawyers or escrow agents, to facilitate or enforce agreements.

Smart contracts utilize cryptographic mechanisms to provide security and enforceability. Once a smart contract is implemented on a blockchain, it becomes tamper-proof and transparent, allowing all parties to verify its execution and outcomes. This trustless nature of smart contracts has the potential to revolutionize various industries by reducing costs, improving efficiency, and enhancing security.

Smart contracts streamline financial processes by automating the execution and enforcement of agreements. They can be used for a variety of applications, including financial transactions, supply chain management, intellectual property rights, and more. Smart contracts reduce the need for manual intervention, increase operational efficiency, and minimize the potential for errors or disputes.

In financial transactions, smart contracts can automate payment settlements, interest calculations, and collateral management. For instance, in a lending scenario, a smart contract can automatically disburse a loan when predefined conditions, such as creditworthiness or collateral verification, are met. Interest payments and loan repayments can also be automatically executed, ensuring timely and accurate transactions.

Supply chain management can benefit from smart contracts by automating and verifying the movement of goods, ensuring compliance with regulations, and facilitating transparent and auditable record-keeping. Smart contracts can automatically trigger actions, including the releasing of payment or verifying the authenticity of goods, based on predefined conditions and real-time data inputs.

Smart contracts serve as the foundation for decentralized applications (DApps) built on blockchain platforms. DApps leverage smart contracts to enable a range of functionalities, including decentralized exchanges, lending platforms, prediction markets, and more. DApps provide users with a seamless, decentralized, and transparent experience, eliminating the need for intermediaries and empowering individuals to take control of their financial interactions.

Decentralized exchanges (DEXs) are a prime example of DApps that utilize smart contracts to facilitate peer-to-peer asset trading. Instead of relying on a centralized exchange, users can exchange digital assets directly with each other, with smart contracts ensuring the integrity of transactions and asset ownership. Lending platforms built on smart contracts enable peer-to-peer lending, where individuals can lend or borrow digital assets directly from other participants. Smart contracts automate loan origination, interest calculation, and repayment, providing individuals with greater access to credit and flexible lending options.

Decentralized Finance, or DeFi, represents a new frontier in the financial landscape, leveraging blockchain technology to create an open and permissionless ecosystem that operates without intermediaries. DeFi aims to provide individuals with equal access to financial services, enabling them to borrow, lend, trade, and invest in a transparent and decentralized manner.

DeFi platforms allow individuals to lend or borrow digital assets directly from other participants, eliminating the need for traditional intermediaries. By utilizing smart contracts, DeFi lending and borrowing protocols automate loan origination, interest calculation, and repayment, providing individuals with greater access to credit and flexible lending options. Peer-to-peer lending through DeFi platforms empowers individuals whom traditional banking services are not available or who are looking for alternative lending options. It enables borrowers to secure loans quickly and with less bureaucracy, while lenders can earn interest on their idle digital assets.

The forefront of DeFi are decentralized exchanges (DEXs), enabling users to trade digital assets directly with each other without relying on centralized intermediaries. These exchanges leverage smart contracts to automate trade settlements, ensuring that transactions are executed securely, transparently, and without the need for a trusted third party. DEXs provide individuals with greater control over their assets and eliminate the risks associated with centralized exchanges, such as hacks or theft. Through DEXs, users can trade a wide range of digital assets in a peer-to-peer manner, with smart contracts guaranteeing the fairness and integrity of transactions.

Yield farming and liquidity mining are popular practices in the DeFi ecosystem that incentivize participants to contribute liquidity to decentralized protocols. Users can lock their digital assets in liquidity pools and earn additional tokens as rewards. This mechanism promotes liquidity and participation in DeFi protocols while allowing individuals to earn passive income. Yield farming involves providing liquidity to decentralized platforms and earning additional tokens in return. Users can stake their digital assets in liquidity pools, which are utilized for various DeFi activities such as lending, borrowing, or trading. In return, participants receive rewards in the form of additional tokens, often referred to as "yield."

Liquidity mining focuses on providing liquidity to new or emerging DeFi protocols. By contributing digital assets to these protocols, users can earn protocol-specific tokens as rewards. Liquidity mining incentivizes early participation, supports the growth of new DeFi projects, and provides individuals with opportunities to earn rewards on their holdings.

DeFi platforms enable the creation as well as trading of synthetic assets and derivatives on blockchain networks. Synthetic assets replicate the value of real-world assets, such as stocks, commodities, or fiat currencies, on the blockchain. By utilizing smart contracts, individuals can gain exposure to these assets without the need for traditional financial intermediaries. Derivatives, which include options and futures, can also be created and traded on DeFi platforms. Smart contracts facilitate the execution and settlement of these financial instruments, providing individuals with additional investment and risk management opportunities.

Automated Market Making (AMM) is a key component of DeFi platforms that enables liquidity provision and price determination in decentralized exchanges. AMM algorithms utilize smart contracts to automatically match buy and sell orders, ensuring continuous liquidity and efficient asset trading.

Decentralized oracles serve as bridges between blockchain platforms and real-world data. They provide reliable and tamper-proof data feeds that smart contracts can utilize for decision-making and execution. Oracles enable DeFi platforms to access real-time market data, external APIs, and other relevant information needed for various financial operations. AMMs and oracles are critical infrastructure components in the DeFi ecosystem, enhancing liquidity, price discovery, and the overall efficiency of decentralized exchanges and financial applications.

While smart contracts and DeFi offer significant opportunities, several challenges and considerations must be addressed to ensure their widespread adoption and effectiveness.

Smart contracts are subject to vulnerabilities and bugs, which can lead to financial losses or exploits. Rigorous code auditing, security best practices, and thorough testing are essential to mitigate these risks. Additionally, establishing robust security standards and protocols within the DeFi ecosystem is crucial to protect user funds and maintain confidence in the system.

As DeFi applications and protocols mature, regulatory compliance becomes an important consideration. The evolving regulatory landscape may require DeFi platforms to adhere to financial regulations, such as anti-money laundering (AML) and know-your-customer (KYC) requirements. Striking a balance between maintaining decentralized principles and complying with regulatory frameworks will be crucial for the sustainable growth of DeFi.

Scalability remains a challenge for blockchain networks, as high transaction volumes can lead to network congestion and increased fees. Innovations such as layer-two solutions and interoperability protocols aim to address scalability issues and enable seamless communication between different blockchain networks, facilitating broader adoption and improving user experience.

- **Cross-border payments and remittances**

Cross-border payments and remittances play a vital role in the global economy, facilitating the movement of funds between individuals and businesses across different countries. However, traditional cross-border payment systems often suffer from inefficiencies, high costs, long settlement times, and limited accessibility. Blockchain technology has emerged as a disruptive solution to these challenges, offering a decentralized, transparent, and efficient framework for cross-border payments and remittances.

Traditional cross-border payment systems encounter several challenges that hinder efficiency and accessibility.

Cross-border transactions often involve multiple intermediaries, such as correspondent banks and clearinghouses, resulting in high fees and unfavorable exchange rates. These costs disproportionately affect individuals and businesses, particularly those in developing countries who heavily rely on remittances.

Traditional cross-border payment systems rely on a complex web of correspondent banking relationships, leading to lengthy settlement times. It can take several days or even weeks for funds to reach their destination, causing delays and impacting business operations and personal finances.

Opaque payment processes and limited visibility into transaction status and fees create mistrust and uncertainty for both senders and recipients. The lack of transparency makes it challenging to track and verify cross-border transactions, increasing the risk of fraud or errors.

Blockchain technology presents a decentralized, secure, and transparent framework for cross-border payments and remittances, addressing the challenges faced by traditional systems.

Blockchain enables direct peer-to-peer transactions without the need for intermediaries. By leveraging smart contracts, funds can be transferred instantly and securely between parties, eliminating the delays and costs associated with traditional banking systems. The decentralized nature of blockchain guarantees that transactions are settled directly between the involved parties, bypassing the need for intermediaries and reducing costs. Moreover, the utilization of cryptocurrencies as a medium of exchange in cross-border payments eliminates the need for expensive currency conversions and facilitates efficient transactions across borders.

Blockchain-based cross-border payments significantly reduce costs by eliminating intermediaries and associated fees. The removal of intermediaries streamlines the payment process, allowing for faster and more cost-effective transfers. Additionally, blockchain's automated and programmable nature reduces manual intervention, improving operational efficiency and reducing the potential for errors. With blockchain, cross-border payment transactions can be settled in near real-time, eliminating the delays caused by traditional banking processes. This increased efficiency benefits individuals and businesses alike, allowing for faster access to funds and enabling smoother global trade.

Blockchain provides transparency and auditability, enhancing trust and accountability in cross-border payments. Transaction records are stored on a distributed ledger, enabling participants to track and verify the movement of funds in real-time. The immutable nature of blockchain ensures transaction integrity and minimizes the danger of fraud or manipulation. Blockchain's transparency and auditability enable participants to view transaction details, including timestamps, amounts, and wallet addresses, ensuring that all participants have access to accurate and verifiable information. This transparency not only instills trust in the payment process but also enables improved regulatory compliance and reduces the potential for illicit activities.

Blockchain technology has been applied in various use cases, transforming cross-border payments and remittances.

Blockchain-based remittance services offer a more efficient and cost-effective alternative to traditional remittance providers. By leveraging blockchain's peer-to-peer nature, individuals can send and receive funds globally with reduced fees and faster settlement times. This empowers individuals, particularly those in underserved regions, to access affordable remittance services and retain more of their hard-earned money. Blockchain-based remittance platforms utilize cryptocurrencies as a medium of exchange, enabling direct and secure transactions between senders and recipients. These platforms leverage smart contracts to automate the remittance process, eliminating the need for intermediaries and providing a seamless experience for users.

Blockchain streamlines cross-border business payments, enabling faster and more transparent transactions. Smart contracts facilitate the automatic execution of payment terms, ensuring timely settlement upon meeting predefined conditions. This reduces the reliance on intermediaries and minimizes administrative burdens, allowing businesses to operate more efficiently and securely in the global marketplace. Blockchain-based business payment platforms provide a secure and transparent environment for cross-border transactions. Smart contracts automate payment processes, ensuring that funds are released to the recipient once the predetermined conditions are met. This eliminates the need for manual verification and reconciliation, streamlining the payment process and reducing the potential for disputes.

Blockchain technology can enhance international trade finance by providing a secure and transparent platform for trade-related transactions. Smart contracts automate processes such as letters of credit, bill of lading, and customs documentation, reducing paperwork, increasing efficiency, and minimizing the risk of fraud. Blockchain-based trade finance platforms enable parties to track and verify the authenticity of goods and facilitate seamless cross-border trade. By leveraging blockchain's distributed ledger technology, international trade finance platforms provide a single source of truth for all trade-related documentation. This eliminates the need for manual document verification, reduces the danger of fraud, and speeds up the trade finance process, benefiting both buyers and sellers.

Several central banks are exploring the development of Central Bank Digital Currencies (CBDCs) using blockchain technology. CBDCs have the ability to streamline cross-border payments by providing a digital representation of fiat currency that can be instantly transferred between participants. CBDCs offer advantages such as reduced settlement times, enhanced security, and increased financial inclusion, while maintaining regulatory oversight. CBDCs built on blockchain technology can facilitate cross-border payments by eliminating the need for intermediaries, reducing costs, and providing real-time settlement. These digital currencies can be seamlessly transferred between participants, enabling efficient and secure cross-border transactions while maintaining regulatory compliance.

While blockchain technology offers promising solutions for cross-border payments and remittances, there are challenges to overcome and factors to consider for wider adoption.

Establishing clear and flexible regulatory frameworks that accommodate blockchain-based payment systems is essential. Regulators must strike a balance between ensuring consumer protection, preventing illicit activities, and fostering innovation. Collaborative efforts between industry stakeholders, governments, and regulatory bodies can help create a conducive environment for blockchain adoption. Regulatory frameworks should address issues such as anti-money laundering (AML) and know-your-customer (KYC) compliance, consumer protection, privacy concerns, and cross-border regulations. Cooperation between regulators and blockchain industry participants is crucial to develop effective regulatory frameworks that promote innovation while safeguarding the integrity of cross-border payments.

Blockchain networks must address scalability issues to handle high transaction volumes required for cross-border payments. As blockchain adoption increases, the capacity to process a large number of transactions becomes paramount. Innovations such as layer-two solutions, sharding, and interoperability protocols are being developed to improve scalability and facilitate seamless communication between different blockchain networks. Interoperability between blockchain networks is vital for the widespread adoption of blockchain-based cross-border payment systems. Standardization efforts and the development of interoperability protocols enable different blockchain platforms to communicate and interact seamlessly, facilitating cross-border transactions and fostering network effects.

Creating user-friendly interfaces and simplifying the onboarding process will be crucial for mainstream adoption of blockchain-based cross-border payment systems. The user experience should be intuitive, ensuring that individuals and businesses can easily navigate the platforms, understand the transaction process, and manage their digital assets. Education and awareness campaigns are necessary to help individuals and businesses understand the benefits, functionality, and security aspects of blockchain-based cross-border payments and remittances. Clear communication about the advantages of blockchain technology, such as cost savings, faster settlement times, and increased transparency, will drive user adoption and confidence in the system.

Supply Chain Management and Logistics

- **Traceability and transparency in supply chains**

Supply chains form the backbone of global trade, connecting manufacturers, distributors, retailers, and consumers across the world. However, traditional supply chain management systems often struggle with maintaining traceability and transparency, leading to challenges such as counterfeit products, lack of accountability, and inefficiencies.

Traditional supply chain management systems encounter several challenges that hinder traceability and transparency.

Many supply chains lack transparency due to the involvement of multiple intermediaries, making it difficult to track the origin, movement, and authenticity of products. This opacity increases the risk of counterfeit products, unethical practices, and regulatory non-compliance.

Supply chain records are often fragmented and stored in different systems, making it challenging to establish a comprehensive and trustworthy audit trail. This fragmentation results in inefficiencies, delays in identifying and addressing issues, and difficulties in conducting effective recalls or investigations.

Accountability is a significant concern in supply chains, especially when it comes to labor practices, environmental impact, and product authenticity. The absence of a transparent and immutable record of activities makes it challenging to hold responsible parties accountable for non-compliance or unethical practices.

Blockchain technology offers a decentralized, secure, and transparent framework for supply chain management, addressing the challenges faced by traditional systems.

Blockchain enables the development of a transparent, immutable ledger that tracks all transactions and product movements along the supply chain. Each transaction is added as a block to the chain, creating a permanent and auditable record of all activities. By leveraging blockchain's distributed ledger technology, supply chain participants can trace the origin, authenticity, and movement of products from their source to the end consumer. This enhanced traceability facilitates faster identification of issues, reduces the risk of counterfeit products, and enables more efficient recalls and investigations.

Blockchain promotes transparency by allowing all parties in the supply chain to have access to the same set of data. This shared and decentralized ledger ensures that information is accurate, tamper-proof, and visible to all authorized parties. Transparency enables supply chain stakeholders, including consumers, to verify the authenticity and ethical sourcing of products. By providing a clear and immutable record of activities, blockchain technology increases accountability, making it easier to identify and address non-compliance, unethical practices, or deviations from established standards.

Smart contracts, programmable agreements executed on the blockchain, automate supply chain processes and enforce predefined rules and conditions. These contracts can automate tasks such as inventory management, quality control, and payments, reducing manual intervention and improving efficiency. Smart contracts enable automated verification of compliance and quality standards, ensuring that products meet specific criteria before progressing along the supply chain. This automation streamlines processes, reduces administrative overheads, and minimizes the risk of human error or manipulation.

Blockchain technology has been applied in various use cases, transforming supply chain management and promoting traceability and transparency.

Blockchain-based solutions have been implemented to enhance food traceability, allowing consumers to track the journey of food products from farm to table. By scanning a product's QR code or using a unique identifier, consumers can access information about the product's origin, production methods, and transportation. Blockchain provides a trusted and immutable record of every step in the supply chain, enabling consumers to verify the authenticity, safety, and ethical practices associated with food products. This level of transparency empowers consumers to make informed choices and supports efforts to combat food fraud and improve food safety.

Blockchain technology is being utilized to promote ethical practices and sustainability in supply chains. By leveraging blockchain's transparency and immutability, organizations can track the sourcing of raw materials, verify compliance with labor and environmental standards, and ensure fair trade practices. Blockchain-based platforms enable supply chain participants to record and share information related to labor conditions, certifications, and environmental impact. This information can be independently verified, promoting ethical sourcing and responsible production practices. Consumers can also access this information, empowering them to support companies that prioritize social and environmental responsibility.

The pharmaceutical industry faces challenges related to counterfeit drugs and the integrity of the supply chain. Blockchain offers a robust solution by providing a tamper-proof and transparent ledger that records the movement of pharmaceutical products. With blockchain, each pharmaceutical product can be assigned a unique identifier or a serial number that is recorded on the blockchain. This enables stakeholders to trace the entire journey of a drug, from manufacturing to distribution, ensuring its authenticity and reducing the risk of counterfeit products entering the market.

Blockchain technology has been applied in the fashion and luxury goods industry to promote transparency and combat counterfeiting. By using blockchain, manufacturers can register their products on a transparent ledger, providing consumers with proof of authenticity and the product's origin. Blockchain allows consumers to verify the authenticity and ethical practices associated with fashion and luxury goods. By scanning a product's unique identifier, consumers can access information about the materials used, manufacturing processes, and certifications, ensuring they are purchasing genuine and ethically produced items.

While blockchain technology offers significant potential for supply chain management, there are challenges to overcome and factors to consider for wider adoption.

Interoperability between different blockchain platforms and existing supply chain systems is crucial for seamless data exchange and collaboration. Efforts to develop interoperability protocols and industry standards will facilitate the integration of blockchain technology into existing supply chain management systems.

Maintaining data privacy and security is essential when implementing blockchain in supply chain management. Confidential business information and sensitive data should be protected, and access to information should be granted based on the principles of permissioned blockchains.

Scalability remains a challenge for blockchain networks, particularly when dealing with large-scale supply chains involving numerous transactions and participants. Innovations such as layer-two solutions and consensus mechanisms need to be developed to ensure the scalability and efficiency required for widespread adoption.

Educating supply chain stakeholders about the benefits and potential applications of blockchain technology is essential for fostering adoption. Collaboration between industry players, governments, and technology providers is crucial for developing blockchain-based solutions that cater to the specific needs of different supply chains.

- **Enhancing efficiency and reducing fraud**

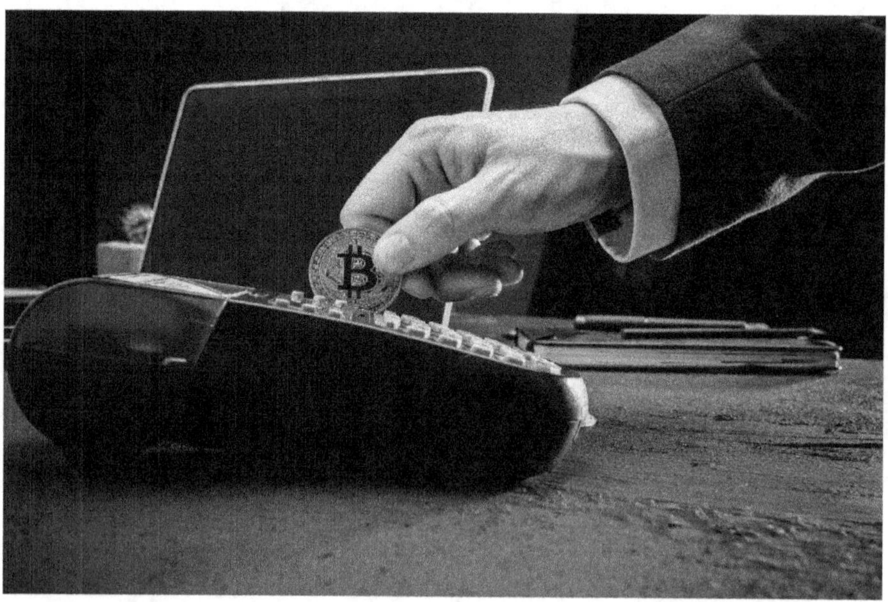

Efficiency and fraud prevention are critical factors in various sectors, including finance, supply chain management, and public administration. Traditional systems often struggle with inefficiencies, lack of transparency, and vulnerability to fraudulent activities. Blockchain technology has emerged as a transformative solution to these challenges, offering a decentralized, transparent, and secure framework that enhances efficiency and reduces fraud.

Traditional systems suffer from inefficiencies that hinder productivity and increase costs. Many industries rely on complex and manual processes that are time-consuming and prone to errors. These processes often involve multiple intermediaries and require extensive reconciliation, resulting in delays, inefficiencies, and increased operational costs.

Traditional systems lack transparency and fail to provide a single source of truth for shared data. This limitation leads to discrepancies, disputes, and the need for extensive reconciliation, causing delays and inefficiencies.

Traditional systems heavily rely on intermediaries such as banks, clearinghouses, or auditors to validate and authenticate transactions. The involvement of multiple intermediaries introduces additional costs, delays, and potential points of failure or manipulation.

Blockchain technology offers innovative solutions to enhance efficiency and streamline operations. Blockchain enables direct peer-to-peer transactions without the need for intermediaries. This decentralization reduces complexity, eliminates delays, and lowers transaction costs, resulting in enhanced efficiency. By leveraging smart contracts, blockchain automates and enforces predefined rules and conditions, facilitating seamless and instant transactions. The elimination of middlemen and the automation of processes significantly improve operational efficiency and reduce administrative burdens.

Blockchain's distributed ledger technology provides a shared, immutable, and transparent record of all transactions. Every transaction is recorded in a block that is linked to previous blocks, creating a secure and auditable history of activities. The transparency and immutability of blockchain ensure data integrity and eliminate the need for extensive reconciliation processes. Participants can access and verify information in real-time, reducing delays, disputes, and errors.

Supply chain management could be transformed by blockchain by increasing efficiency, traceability, and transparency. Each phase of the chain of supply, from sourcing materials through manufacturing, distribution, and delivery, may be recorded and tracked by stakeholders using blockchain. This enhanced visibility enables proactive monitoring, reduces delays, improves inventory management, and enhances collaboration between supply chain participants.

Smart contracts on blockchain platforms automate processes such as purchase orders, invoicing, and inventory management, streamlining operations and reducing the reliance on manual intervention. The automation of these processes minimizes errors, improves accuracy, and speeds up the overall supply chain.

Blockchain technology offers robust solutions to combat fraud, enhancing security and trust. Blockchain's immutability ensures that once a transaction is recorded, it cannot be altered or deleted. This feature provides an immutable audit trail, making it challenging for malicious actors to manipulate or falsify records. The transparency and accountability of blockchain allow participants to verify the integrity of transactions and ensure compliance with established rules and regulations. The immutability of blockchain records acts as a deterrent to fraudulent activities.

Blockchain can enhance identity verification processes, reducing the risk of identity theft and fraud. Through blockchain-based identity management systems, individuals can maintain control over their personal data, granting permission to specific entities to access their information. By leveraging cryptographic algorithms, blockchain ensures secure and tamper-proof identity verification. This reduces the reliance on traditional authentication methods, which are often susceptible to fraudulent activities.

Smart contracts on blockchain platforms can play a crucial role in preventing fraud. These programmable contracts automatically execute predefined rules and conditions, eliminating the need for manual intervention and reducing the risk of fraudulent activities. Smart contracts can be designed to enforce compliance, verify identities, and ensure the authenticity of transactions. By automating these processes, blockchain minimizes human error and reduces opportunities for fraud.

Blockchain technology has been applied across various industries to enhance efficiency and reduce fraud. Blockchain has the potential to streamline financial services, including payments, remittances, and identity verification. Through decentralized platforms, financial transactions can be executed directly between parties, eliminating intermediaries, reducing costs, and increasing transaction speed. Blockchain-based identity verification systems enhance security, making it difficult for fraudsters to manipulate personal information. The transparency and immutability of blockchain records help prevent identity theft and fraudulent financial activities.

Blockchain enhances supply chain efficiency by improving transparency, traceability, and accountability. Through decentralized and immutable ledgers, supply chain participants can track and validate the movement of goods, ensuring authenticity, as well as reducing the risk of counterfeit products. By automating processes through smart contracts, blockchain minimizes errors, delays, and fraudulent activities. This streamlined supply chain management reduces costs, enhances operational efficiency, and promotes trust between stakeholders.

Blockchain technology can revolutionize government and public administration by improving transparency, efficiency, and data security. Blockchain-based systems can streamline administrative processes, such as land registration, voting systems, and public procurement. Blockchain's transparency and immutability reduce corruption and ensure the integrity of public records. Smart contracts can automate government processes, minimizing bureaucracy and enhancing efficiency.

While blockchain technology offers significant potential for enhancing efficiency and reducing fraud, several challenges need to be addressed for widespread adoption.

Blockchain networks must overcome scalability limitations to handle large volumes of transactions. Innovations such as sharding and layer-two solutions are being developed to improve blockchain's scalability. Interoperability between different blockchain platforms and existing systems is crucial for seamless data exchange and collaboration. Standardization efforts and interoperability protocols are being developed to facilitate integration across various blockchain networks.

Establishing clear and flexible regulatory frameworks is essential to address legal and compliance concerns associated with blockchain adoption. Regulations should strike a balance between fostering innovation and ensuring consumer protection.

Education and awareness about blockchain technology are crucial for its widespread adoption. Collaborative efforts between industry players, government agencies, and educational institutions can promote understanding and exploration of blockchain's potential applications.

- **Case studies of successful implementations**

Blockchain technology has appeared as a disruptive force with the potential to revolutionize various industries. While its theoretical benefits are widely discussed, understanding real-world applications and successful implementations is crucial to assess its practical value.

The finance and banking sector has been at the forefront of blockchain adoption, with successful implementations demonstrating enhanced efficiency and improved services.

Ripple, a blockchain-based payment protocol, has revolutionized cross-border payments. Through its network and cryptocurrency XRP, Ripple enables financial institutions to settle international transactions in real-time, bypassing the traditional correspondent banking system. This has significantly reduced settlement times and lowered transaction costs, benefiting both banks and end-users. Ripple's success lies in its ability to address the inefficiencies and delays associated with traditional cross-border payments. By providing a decentralized platform that eliminates the need for multiple intermediaries, Ripple has streamlined the process, enhanced transparency, and increased the speed of transactions.

JPMorgan Chase, one of the world's largest financial institutions, implemented the Interbank Information Network (IIN), a blockchain-based solution aimed at improving the efficiency of correspondent banking. IIN allows member banks to securely share information, verify data in real-time, and address compliance-related challenges. The implementation of IIN has resulted in significant improvements in operational efficiency and cost reduction. By streamlining the Know Your Customer (KYC) process and reducing delays in information sharing, IIN has enhanced collaboration among banks, reduced duplicative efforts, and improved overall efficiency in correspondent banking.

Blockchain technology has immense potential to transform supply chain management by enhancing transparency, traceability, and efficiency.

Walmart, in collaboration with IBM, implemented a blockchain solution for food traceability. By utilizing blockchain technology, Walmart can track the journey of products from farm to store shelves, ensuring transparency and accountability. This solution has improved food safety, reduced response times during recalls, and enhanced consumer trust in the quality and authenticity of Walmart's products. The blockchain-based system allows for the seamless recording and verification of every step in the supply chain, ensuring the integrity and authenticity of products. This level of transparency empowers consumers to make informed choices and holds suppliers accountable for their practices.

Maersk, the world's largest shipping company, partnered with IBM to develop TradeLens, a blockchain platform for global supply chain management. TradeLens provides end-to-end visibility, automates documentation processes, and facilitates secure data sharing among supply chain stakeholders. The implementation of TradeLens has transformed the efficiency of global trade by reducing paperwork, enhancing transparency, and streamlining operations. Through the blockchain platform, participants can securely share and access real-time information, resulting in improved collaboration, reduced errors, and increased trust among supply chain partners.

Blockchain technology offers solutions to the challenges faced by the healthcare industry, such as data interoperability, privacy, and security.

Estonia has successfully implemented blockchain technology in its healthcare system to secure and manage electronic health records (EHRs). The blockchain-based system ensures the integrity and privacy of patient data while allowing authorized healthcare providers to access and update records securely. The implementation of blockchain in Estonia's healthcare system has led to improved patient care coordination, reduced administrative burdens, and increased patient trust in the security of their health information. The decentralized nature of blockchain ensures that patient data remains secure, while healthcare providers can access the necessary information for informed decision-making.

MedRec, a blockchain-based system developed by researchers at MIT, aims to address the challenges of medical data sharing and interoperability. MedRec enables patients to have control over their medical records and grant access to healthcare providers as needed. The decentralized approach to medical data sharing through blockchain ensures patient privacy, reduces redundant tests and procedures, and facilitates research collaboration among institutions. MedRec has the potential to improve patient outcomes, reduce healthcare costs, and foster innovation in the healthcare industry.

Governments worldwide are exploring the applications of blockchain technology to enhance the efficiency, transparency, and security of public services.

Dubai's government has implemented a comprehensive blockchain strategy to enhance government services across various sectors. Blockchain is utilized for land registration, visa applications, business registration, and other administrative processes. The implementation of blockchain in Dubai has led to reduced paperwork, improved data security, and increased operational efficiency. The decentralized and transparent nature of blockchain ensures the integrity of public records, reduces bureaucratic processes, and enhances citizen trust in government services.

Sweden is leveraging blockchain technology to explore secure and self-sovereign digital identities for its citizens. By utilizing blockchain, Sweden aims to provide individuals with control over their personal data while enabling seamless interactions with government services. The implementation of blockchain for digital identity management in Sweden enhances privacy, reduces the risk of identity fraud, and streamlines access to government services. Citizens can securely access and share their personal data, simplifying administrative procedures and enhancing the overall user experience.

While these case studies highlight successful blockchain implementations, challenges remain in terms of scalability, interoperability, regulatory frameworks, and public awareness. Overcoming these challenges will be crucial for wider blockchain adoption and realizing its full potential. Scalability is a key challenge that blockchain networks must address to handle large transaction volumes without compromising performance. Innovations such as sharding, layer-two solutions, and consensus mechanisms are being developed to enhance scalability.

Interoperability between different blockchain platforms and existing systems is essential for seamless data exchange and collaboration. Standardization efforts and interoperability protocols are being developed to facilitate integration across various blockchain networks. Regulatory frameworks are vital in ensuring compliance, protecting consumer rights, and fostering innovation. Governments and regulatory bodies are required to establish clear and flexible regulations that strike a balance between encouraging blockchain adoption and addressing concerns such as data privacy, security, and financial regulations.

Public awareness and education about blockchain technology are crucial for widespread adoption. Collaboration between industry players, academic institutions, and government agencies can drive research, development, and the dissemination of blockchain knowledge. The future potential of blockchain technology is vast. It can revolutionize industries such as voting systems, intellectual property rights, supply chain finance, and more. Moreover, advancements in blockchain scalability, privacy-preserving techniques, and interoperability protocols will further enhance its capabilities and drive innovation.

Healthcare and Pharmaceutical Industry

- **Securing medical records and data privacy**

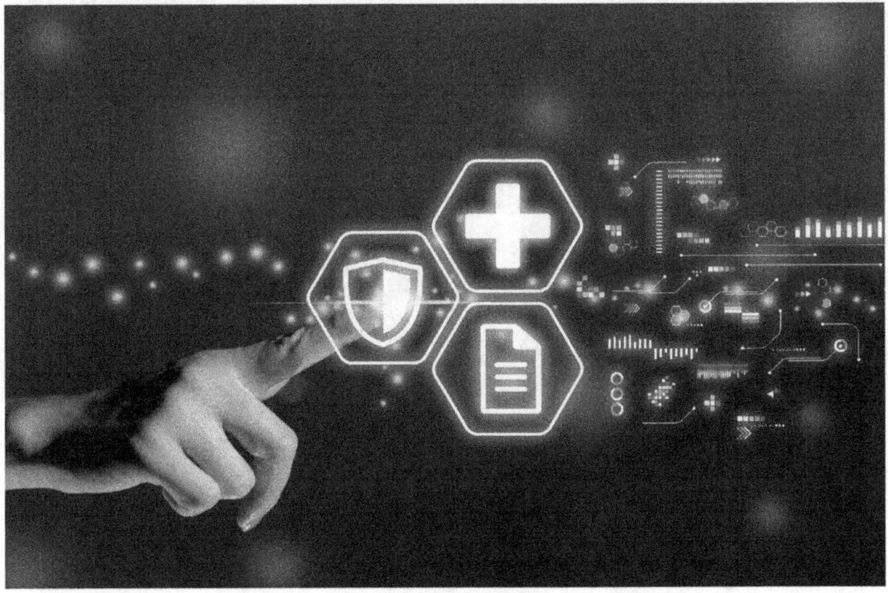

The healthcare industry faces significant challenges in securing patient medical records and protecting data privacy. Traditional systems often struggle with vulnerabilities, data breaches, and fragmented information silos, compromising patient confidentiality and hindering efficient healthcare

The security as well as privacy of medical records are two issues that the healthcare business must contend with.

Traditional centralized systems store medical records in centralized databases, making them vulnerable to cyberattacks and data breaches. Hacking incidents can compromise the confidentiality, integrity, and availability of patient data, resulting in identity theft, medical fraud, and other detrimental consequences.

Healthcare providers often use disparate systems that lack interoperability, leading to fragmented information silos. This fragmentation makes it difficult to share patient data securely and efficiently, hindering seamless healthcare delivery and impeding medical research and innovation.

Patients frequently have limited control over their medical records and lack transparency regarding who accesses their data. The current consent process for sharing medical information is cumbersome and lacks transparency, impeding patient engagement and autonomy.

Blockchain technology offers a decentralized, immutable, and secure framework for securing medical records and addressing the challenges faced by traditional systems.

Blockchain's distributed ledger technology allows medical records to be stored across a network of computers rather than a single centralized server. This decentralized approach eliminates the vulnerability of a single point of failure, making it challenging for hackers to compromise the entire system. Additionally, blockchain's immutability ensures that once a transaction is recorded, it cannot be altered, providing an auditable and tamper-proof record of medical data.

Blockchain employs advanced cryptographic techniques to protect medical data. Patient information is encrypted and can only be accessed by authorized individuals with the corresponding private keys. This ensures that patient data remains confidential and secure, reducing the risk of unauthorized access and data breaches.

Blockchain technology enables patients to have greater control over their medical records. Through smart contracts, patients can grant or revoke consent for specific healthcare providers or researchers to access their data. This ensures transparency and gives patients the ability to actively participate in the sharing of their medical information.

Blockchain technology has been successfully employed in various healthcare use cases, showcasing its potential to secure medical records and protect data privacy.

Estonia has implemented blockchain technology for its electronic health records (EHR) system. Blockchain ensures the integrity and security of patient data while allowing authorized healthcare providers to access and update records securely. Patients have control over their EHRs and can grant access to healthcare providers as needed. This implementation has improved patient care coordination, reduced administrative burdens, and increased patient trust in the security of their health information.

MedRec, a blockchain-based system developed by researchers at MIT, focuses on securing medical data and enhancing patient privacy. MedRec allows patients to maintain control over their medical records and grant access to healthcare providers for specific purposes. The decentralized nature of MedRec ensures that patient data remains secure, while healthcare providers can access the necessary information for informed decision-making. This implementation reduces redundant tests and procedures, improves care coordination, and enables research collaboration while maintaining patient privacy.

While blockchain technology shows promise in securing medical records and data privacy, there are challenges and considerations to address for widespread adoption.

Interoperability between different blockchain platforms and existing healthcare systems is crucial for seamless data exchange and collaboration. Developing interoperability standards and protocols is essential to ensure compatibility and efficient sharing of medical records across different institutions.

Blockchain networks need to overcome scalability limitations to handle large volumes of medical data as well as transactions. Advancements in blockchain technologies, such as sharding and layer-two solutions, are being explored to address scalability and performance challenges.

Establishing clear regulatory and legal frameworks is essential to address concerns related to privacy, data protection, and compliance in the healthcare industry. Governments and regulatory bodies need to work collaboratively to develop frameworks that strike a balance between protecting patient privacy and enabling innovative uses of blockchain technology.

Widespread adoption of blockchain technology in healthcare requires educating stakeholders and healthcare professionals about its benefits and addressing concerns related to integration, costs, and training. Collaborative efforts between technology providers, healthcare organizations, and policymakers are crucial to promote awareness, understanding, and seamless integration of blockchain solutions.

- **Clinical trials and drug supply chain management**

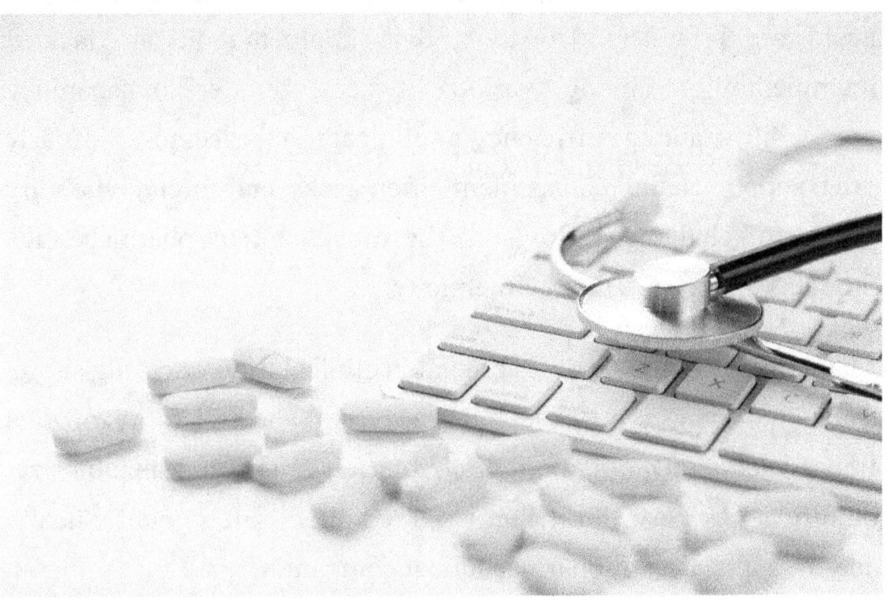

Clinical trials and drug supply chain management are pivotal components of the healthcare industry, involving complex processes, stringent regulations, and the need for transparency, traceability, and data integrity. Traditional systems in these areas often struggle with challenges such as data fragmentation, lack of transparency, and inefficient processes, leading to delays, errors, and potential risks to patient safety. However, blockchain technology offers a transformative solution by providing a decentralized, transparent, and secure framework.

Clinical trials and drug supply chain management face significant challenges that hinder their efficiency and effectiveness.

Clinical trials involve the collection and analysis of huge amounts of data from various sources, including patients, researchers, and healthcare providers. However, data fragmentation and lack of interoperability among various systems hinder transparency, accessibility, and the efficiency of clinical trial processes. Similarly, drug supply chain management often lacks end-to-end visibility, making it challenging to track the movement of pharmaceutical products and ensure their authenticity.

Maintaining data integrity is crucial in clinical trials and drug supply chain management to ensure the accuracy and reliability of data. Issues such as data tampering, counterfeit drugs, and unauthorized modifications pose significant risks to patient safety, public health, and the reputation of pharmaceutical companies.

Both clinical trials and drug supply chain management require compliance with stringent regulations and auditing processes. Ensuring adherence to regulatory requirements, verifying the authenticity of data, and conducting audits can be time-consuming, costly, and prone to errors in traditional systems.

A decentralized, unaltered ledger made possible by blockchain technology protects the accuracy and traceability of clinical trial data. Every transaction or data entry is recorded in a block and linked to previous blocks, creating a transparent and auditable history of activities. This transparency and immutability enhance data integrity, making it challenging for unauthorized parties to tamper with or manipulate data. Blockchain's distributed ledger ensures that all stakeholders have access to a shared source of truth, eliminating the fragmentation of data. This enhances transparency and collaboration among researchers, healthcare providers, and regulatory bodies, facilitating more efficient and reliable clinical trial processes.

Blockchain has the potential to streamline patient recruitment for clinical trials by securely matching eligible patients with relevant trials. Through self-sovereign identities stored on the blockchain, patients can maintain control over their personal information and grant consent for data sharing. This streamlines the consent process, enhances patient privacy, and facilitates the efficient identification of suitable candidates for clinical trials. By leveraging blockchain's secure and decentralized nature, patient data can be encrypted and kept on the blockchain, ensuring confidentiality and data protection. Smart contracts can automate the consent process, allowing patients to grant or revoke access to their data with transparency and control.

Blockchain enables secure data sharing and collaboration among stakeholders involved in clinical trials, including researchers, pharmaceutical companies, regulatory bodies, and patients. By utilizing smart contracts, access to sensitive data can be regulated, and predefined rules and conditions can be enforced automatically. This enhances data privacy and security while promoting efficient collaboration and ensuring compliance with data sharing agreements. Blockchain's cryptographic techniques ensure that sensitive data is encrypted and only accessible to authorized participants. The decentralized nature of blockchain also reduces the reliance on central authorities, giving individuals more control over their data and increasing trust among stakeholders.

Blockchain provides end-to-end visibility and traceability in the drug supply chain by recording every transaction, movement, and change of ownership on the blockchain. This enables stakeholders to track the origin, authenticity, and movement of pharmaceutical products, reducing the risk of counterfeit drugs entering the supply chain. Blockchain ensures transparency by creating an immutable record of every transaction, including the details of drug manufacturers, distributors, and retailers. This transparency allows regulators and consumers to verify the authenticity and integrity of pharmaceutical products, ensuring patient safety and minimizing the impact of counterfeit drugs.

Blockchain streamlines track and trace processes by automating the recording and verification of drug-related data, such as manufacturing details, batch numbers, and expiration dates. This automation eliminates the reliance on manual processes and paper-based documentation, reducing errors, delays, and the risk of counterfeit drugs that are entering the supply chain. Through blockchain-enabled systems, each transaction in the drug supply chain is recorded and time-stamped, creating an auditable and tamper-proof history of the product's journey. This facilitates efficient recalls, improves inventory management, and enhances the overall efficiency of the drug supply chain.

Counterfeit drugs pose a significant threat to patient safety and public health. Blockchain technology can enhance drug authentication and anti-counterfeiting measures by providing a decentralized and immutable ledger that verifies the authenticity of pharmaceutical products. Through unique identifiers and serialization data recorded on the blockchain, stakeholders can verify the integrity of drug supply chains and identify counterfeit products. Blockchain-based solutions, such as smart tags or NFC (Near Field Communication) chips, can be used to authenticate drug packaging and ensure its integrity. By scanning the unique identifier, consumers and healthcare providers can access information stored on the blockchain, verifying the authenticity of the product and confirming its compliance with regulatory standards.

Despite the potential benefits, several challenges need to be addressed for the widespread utilization of blockchain technology in clinical trials and drug supply chain management.

Ensuring interoperability and standardization of blockchain platforms and systems is crucial for widespread adoption and seamless integration within the healthcare industry. Collaborative efforts and industry-wide initiatives are needed to establish common frameworks, protocols, and data exchange standards. Interoperability will facilitate the efficient sharing of data among different stakeholders and systems, enhancing the overall effectiveness of clinical trials and drug supply chain management.

Scalability remains a challenge for blockchain networks, particularly in handling the volume of transactions and data generated in clinical trials and drug supply chain management. Innovations such as sharding, layer-two solutions, and consensus mechanisms are being explored to address scalability concerns and improve the performance of blockchain networks. These advancements will be critical for handling the 66 ncreaseing demands of data-intensive processes in healthcare.

Regulatory frameworks need to adapt to the evolving nature of blockchain technology, ensuring compliance with existing regulations while providing guidelines for new applications. Collaboration between regulatory bodies, industry stakeholders, and technology developers is essential to establish frameworks that foster innovation while addressing concerns related to data privacy, security, and legal compliance. Regulations should strike a balance between protecting patient privacy, ensuring data security, and fostering the responsible use of blockchain in clinical trials and drug supply chain management.

Education and awareness about blockchain technology are crucial for its successful adoption in clinical trials and drug supply chain management. Training programs, workshops, and collaborations between industry players, researchers, and healthcare professionals can promote understanding and foster adoption. Building knowledge and expertise in blockchain technology will empower stakeholders to explore its potential applications, address challenges, and drive innovation in the healthcare industry.

- **Improving patient care and interoperability**

The healthcare industry is increasingly adopting digital technologies to enhance patient care, streamline processes, and improve outcomes. Among these technologies, blockchain stands out as a transformative innovation that offers secure, decentralized, and interoperable solutions.

The healthcare industry faces challenges related to fragmented health data and communication among various healthcare providers and systems. Patient information is often scattered across multiple healthcare institutions, making it difficult to achieve a comprehensive view of a patient's medical history. This fragmentation hinders care coordination, increases the risk of medical errors, and limits the ability to provide personalized and efficient care.

Traditional healthcare systems often suffer from inefficiencies and a lack of trust in data integrity. Manual processes, paper-based records, and siloed information systems contribute to delays, errors, and miscommunication. These challenges hinder the seamless exchange of information among healthcare providers, compromising patient care and impeding medical advancements.

Blockchain offers a decentralized and secure platform for managing patient health records. Through blockchain technology, patient data can be securely stored, encrypted, and shared across healthcare providers while ensuring data integrity. Blockchain's distributed ledger ensures that patient information remains tamper-proof and accessible only to authorized parties, enhancing data security and privacy.

Blockchain enables seamless interoperability and care coordination among healthcare providers, as it provides a unified and standardized platform for data exchange. With blockchain, healthcare organizations can securely share patient data, including medical records, test results, and treatment plans. This real-time access to comprehensive patient information facilitates informed decision-making, reduces redundant procedures, and improves care coordination across different healthcare settings.

Blockchain technology empowers patients by giving them control over their health data. Through blockchain-enabled platforms, patients can access and manage their medical records, grant consent for data sharing, and participate actively in their own care. This patient-centric approach enhances patient engagement, enables personalized medicine, and promotes better health outcomes.

Blockchain can revolutionize personal health records (PHRs) by providing patients with a secure and comprehensive repository of their health information. Patients can have a complete view of their medical history, including diagnoses, medications, allergies, and procedures, regardless of the healthcare provider. This centralized and interoperable PHR system allows patients to share their information with healthcare providers, ensuring accurate diagnoses, personalized treatments, and seamless care transitions.

Blockchain technology can enhance telemedicine and remote patient monitoring by securely collecting, storing, and sharing patient-generated health data. Through blockchain-enabled platforms, healthcare providers can access real-time patient data, such as vital signs, medication adherence, and lifestyle habits. This enables proactive interventions, remote consultations, and personalized care plans, irrespective of geographical barriers.

Blockchain offers a transformative solution for clinical research and trials by streamlining data management, ensuring data integrity, and enhancing participant recruitment. Through blockchain, researchers can securely access, share, and analyze patient data, accelerating the discovery of new treatments and interventions. Additionally, blockchain facilitates participant recruitment by securely matching eligible patients with clinical trials based on their health data and preferences.

Standardizing data formats and protocols is crucial for achieving interoperability in healthcare. Collaborative efforts among healthcare institutions, technology providers, and regulatory bodies are needed to establish common standards for data exchange and ensure seamless interoperability across different blockchain systems.

Blockchain networks must overcome scalability challenges to handle the increasing volume of healthcare data. Innovations such as sharding, off-chain solutions, and consensus mechanisms are being explored to improve blockchain's scalability and performance, ensuring that it can meet the demands of large-scale healthcare applications.

The implementation of blockchain in healthcare must comply with existing regulations and ethical guidelines to protect patient privacy, ensure data security, and maintain confidentiality. Regulatory bodies need to adapt to the evolving nature of blockchain technology, providing clear guidelines to promote innovation while addressing concerns related to data protection, consent, and governance.

Education and awareness about blockchain technology are crucial for its successful adoption in healthcare. Healthcare professionals, patients, and policymakers need to be educated about the potential benefits and challenges of blockchain, fostering understanding and trust in the technology. Training programs, workshops, and collaborative efforts can support the adoption of blockchain solutions and encourage stakeholders to embrace the transformative potential it offers.

Government and Public Services

- **Identity management and digital voting systems**

Identity management and voting systems are fundamental pillars of modern societies, tasked with ensuring secure and reliable identification and conducting fair and transparent elections. However, traditional systems often struggle to address challenges such as identity theft, fraud, and the lack of transparency. In recent years, blockchain technology has appeared as a transformative solution that offers a decentralized, immutable, and transparent framework for identity management and digital voting systems.

Identity management and digital voting systems face numerous challenges that hinder their effectiveness and integrity:

Traditional identity management systems are centralized and vulnerable to cyberattacks, data breaches, and unauthorized access. These vulnerabilities expose individuals to the risk of identity theft and fraud, compromising their personal information and leading to financial loss, reputational damage, and legal consequences.

Traditional voting systems often lack transparency, making it difficult to ensure the integrity of elections. Issues such as voter fraud, tampering with ballots, and inconsistencies in the counting process erode public trust and confidence in the democratic process. Furthermore, logistical challenges, manual processes, and geographical limitations impede the efficiency and accessibility of elections.

Blockchain technology offers a decentralized and tamper-proof platform for creating secure and verifiable identity credentials. Individuals can store their identity information, such as personal details and biometrics, on a blockchain, ensuring the authenticity and integrity of their identities. Through cryptographic techniques, these credentials can be instantly verified, reducing the risk of identity theft and fraud.

Blockchain empowers individuals with self-sovereign identity, allowing them to control and manage their personal data. With blockchain-based identity solutions, individuals can selectively share their data with trusted parties while maintaining privacy and data ownership. The decentralized nature of blockchain takes away the need for intermediaries, giving individuals greater control over their data and reducing the risk of unauthorized access.

Blockchain simplifies the process of identity verification and authentication by providing a secure and decentralized network for validating identities. Organizations can quickly and securely verify individuals' identities without relying on cumbersome manual processes. This streamlines customer onboarding, reduces fraud, and enhances user experience.

Blockchain technology can revolutionize government-issued digital IDs by providing secure and tamper-proof identity credentials. Individuals can store their identity information on a blockchain, and government agencies can issue digital IDs that are linked to the blockchain. These digital IDs can be used for various purposes, such as accessing government services, participating in online transactions, and proving identity in a secure and verifiable manner.

Blockchain enables cross-organizational identity verification, allowing different entities to collaborate and share identity information securely. For example, financial institutions can validate customer identities using a blockchain-based identity network, reducing duplication of efforts and enhancing the efficiency of Know Your Customer (KYC) processes.

Blockchain provides a transparent and immutable ledger for recording and storing voting records. Each vote is registered as a transaction on the blockchain, creating an auditable and tamper-proof history of the voting process. This transparency ensures that votes cannot be altered or manipulated, increasing trust in the electoral process.

Blockchain technology allows for secure and private voting through cryptographic techniques. Voters can submit their encrypted votes, which are recorded on the blockchain without revealing their identity. This protects voter privacy while maintaining the verifiability and integrity of the voting process.

Blockchain-based voting systems can overcome geographical limitations and increase accessibility. Through online voting platforms built on blockchain technology, voters can cast their votes from anywhere, eliminating the need for physical presence at polling stations. This improves voter turnout, reduces costs, and enhances the efficiency of the electoral process.

The widespread adoption of blockchain in identity management and digital voting systems requires addressing various challenges and considerations:

The successful implementation of blockchain in these domains relies on establishing trust among stakeholders, including individuals, organizations, and governments. Education and awareness campaigns are essential to build trust, explain the benefits, address concerns, and promote the responsible use of blockchain technology.

Scalability remains a challenge for blockchain networks, particularly in handling the high volume of transactions in digital voting systems. Innovations such as sharding, layer-two solutions, and consensus mechanisms are being explored to address scalability concerns and ensure the efficient processing of votes.

Legal and regulatory frameworks need to adapt to the integration of blockchain in identity management and voting systems. Governments must establish clear guidelines and regulations to ensure compliance, protect privacy, and address concerns such as voter eligibility, data protection, and dispute resolution.

While blockchain systems offer enhanced security, they are not immune to cybersecurity threats. Continuous research, development, and collaboration among experts are necessary to identify and mitigate potential risks, ensuring the robustness and security of blockchain-based identity management and voting systems.

- **Blockchain in land registration and property rights**

Land registration and property rights are vital components of any society, providing the foundation for secure ownership, facilitating transactions, and safeguarding property rights. However, traditional land registration systems often face challenges such as fraud, corruption, as well as lack of transparency. In recent years, blockchain technology has appeared as a transformative solution, offering a decentralized, transparent, and immutable framework for land registration and property rights.

The existing land registration and property rights systems encounter several challenges that hinder their effectiveness:

Traditional land registration systems are vulnerable to fraud and corruption, as centralized databases can be tampered with or manipulated. Such activities compromise the integrity of land records, leading to disputes, uncertainty, and loss of property rights.

Transparency issues in land registration make it difficult to verify ownership and create obstacles for property transactions. The absence of a reliable and accessible source of land records creates doubts regarding the legitimacy and accuracy of property rights, eroding trust in the system.

Manual and paper-based processes prevalent in land registration systems contribute to inefficiencies and high transaction costs. Delays in processing transactions, complex paperwork, and bureaucratic hurdles increase the time and resources required for property transfers, impeding economic growth and development.

A decentralized, unaltered ledger made possible by blockchain technology for securely storing land records. Each land transaction, including transfers, sales, and encumbrances, is recorded as a permanent entry on the blockchain. This transparency ensures that all stakeholders have access to an accurate and tamper-proof history of land ownership, thereby eliminating disputes and enhancing trust in property rights.

Blockchain's decentralized nature and cryptographic algorithms provide a robust security framework for land registration. By storing land records on a distributed ledger, blockchain minimizes the risk of unauthorized modifications, fraud, and corruption. Smart contracts can automate verification processes and ensure that property transfers occur only when predefined conditions are met, further reducing the potential for fraudulent activities.

Blockchain streamlines land transactions by automating processes and reducing the need for intermediaries. With blockchain-based platforms, property buyers and sellers can engage in direct peer-to-peer transactions, eliminating the reliance on multiple intermediaries and reducing transaction costs. Smart contracts can facilitate the execution of property agreements, automating tasks such as payment transfers and document verification, leading to faster and more efficient transactions.

Blockchain technology revolutionizes title registration and verification by providing a transparent as well as secure platform for recording land titles. Each title entry on the blockchain includes information such as property boundaries, ownership details, and transaction history. This allows individuals and institutions to easily verify land ownership, streamlining the process and reducing the risk of fraudulent claims.

Blockchain simplifies property transactions and transfers by providing a decentralized and efficient platform for peer-to-peer transactions. Buyers and sellers can execute property agreements using smart contracts, eliminating the requirement for intermediaries and reducing transaction costs. Blockchain ensures transparency, trust, and speed in property transactions, making the process more accessible and efficient.

Blockchain-based land registration systems can facilitate dispute resolution by providing a transparent as well as auditable record of land ownership. In case of disputes, the blockchain's immutable ledger can perform as a dependable source of information, helping to resolve conflicts efficiently and impartially. Additionally, blockchain can improve land governance by enabling more effective monitoring and management of land-related activities, such as zoning, taxation, and land-use planning.

The integration of blockchain in land registration necessitates addressing various challenges and considerations:

To fully leverage the benefits of blockchain in land registration, supportive legal and regulatory frameworks need to be developed. Governments must adapt existing laws to accommodate blockchain technology, ensuring its compatibility with established property rights and addressing issues related to jurisdiction, liability, and enforceability.

To realize the full potential of blockchain in land registration, data standardization and interoperability are crucial. Collaboration among government agencies, land registries, and technology providers is necessary to establish common data formats and protocols, ensuring seamless integration and compatibility across different blockchain platforms.

The successful adoption of blockchain in land registration requires education and capacity building for stakeholders involved. Training programs, awareness campaigns, and technical support initiatives can empower government officials, land administrators, and the general public to understand and embrace blockchain technology, fostering its effective and widespread implementation.

As land registration involves sensitive personal and property information, privacy and data protection are paramount. Blockchain systems must comply with relevant data protection regulations and incorporate privacy-enhancing mechanisms, such as encryption and permissioned access, to ensure the confidentiality and security of land-related data.

- **Combating corruption and ensuring transparency**

Corruption is a pervasive issue that affects societies worldwide, undermining economic development, eroding public trust, and perpetuating social inequalities. Traditional systems have often struggled to effectively combat corruption due to factors such as lack of transparency, centralized control, and limited accountability. However, the appearance of blockchain technology has introduced a potent tool in the fight against corruption.

Corruption has far-reaching consequences, impacting economic stability, investment climate, and social well-being. It diverts resources meant for public services, hampers fair competition, and perpetuates social inequalities. Addressing corruption is vital for sustainable development, promoting economic growth, and fostering social justice.

Transparency serves as a potent tool in combating corruption. By ensuring openness, accountability, and accessibility of information, transparency creates an environment where corrupt practices find it difficult to thrive. Transparent systems promote public trust, enable scrutiny, and empower citizens to hold governments and institutions accountable for their actions.

One of the key features of blockchain is its ability to provide immutable and transparent records. By storing information in a decentralized and tamper-proof ledger, blockchain ensures the integrity and transparency of records. Each transaction recorded on the blockchain forms an unalterable block, creating a transparent and auditable trail that increases accountability and helps expose corrupt practices.

Smart contracts, operating on blockchain technology, enable the implementation of predefined actions when specific conditions are met. These self-executing agreements automate processes, eliminate the need for intermediaries, and ensure transparency and compliance with predetermined rules. Smart contracts can facilitate transparent and corruption-resistant governance systems, reducing the potential for manipulation or unethical practices.

Blockchain operates on a decentralized network where no single entity has control over the entire system. The decentralized nature of blockchain ensures that power is not concentrated in the hands of a few, minimizing the risk of corruption. Trust is established through cryptographic algorithms and consensus mechanisms that validate and secure transactions, creating a trustless environment.

Blockchain technology has the potential to enhance transparency in financial systems, reducing corruption risks. By recording and tracking financial transactions on a distributed ledger, blockchain enables real-time auditing and reduces the possibility of money laundering, bribery, and embezzlement. Transparent financial systems foster accountability, discourage illicit activities, and promote fair and inclusive economies.

Blockchain can transform supply chain management by offering end-to-end transparency. By tracking and recording every step of the supply chain on the blockchain, from raw material sourcing to product delivery, stakeholders can verify the authenticity and integrity of goods, reduce counterfeiting, and mitigate corrupt practices such as bribery and fraud. Transparent supply chains promote fair trade, ethical sourcing, and responsible business practices.

Blockchain can significantly enhance transparent governance by ensuring the accountability of public officials and the integrity of public services. Through blockchain-based voting systems, citizens can participate in elections securely and verifiably, reducing the risk of electoral fraud. Blockchain can also enhance the transparency of public expenditure by recording and tracking government budgets and expenditures, facilitating public scrutiny and deterring corruption.

The widespread adoption of blockchain technology in combating corruption requires cooperation and collaboration among governments, institutions, and stakeholders. Organizations must be willing to embrace blockchain solutions and integrate them into existing systems, ensuring interoperability and compatibility. Education campaigns and awareness initiatives are essential to foster understanding and acceptance of blockchain technology.

To effectively implement blockchain technology in combating corruption, stakeholders need education and awareness regarding its potential and benefits. Building knowledge and expertise around blockchain's intricacies, benefits, and limitations will enable stakeholders to leverage its power in combating corruption effectively. Education campaigns, workshops, and training programs can help build the necessary expertise and knowledge base.

The integration of blockchain technology necessitates the development of supportive legal and regulatory frameworks. Governments must adapt existing laws to accommodate blockchain technology, address concerns related to privacy, data protection, and jurisdiction, and establish clear guidelines for the use of blockchain in combating corruption. Effective legal frameworks will provide a conducive environment for the implementation of blockchain-based solutions.

Blockchain networks must address scalability and efficiency challenges to handle the large volume of transactions associated with combating corruption. Ongoing research and development are necessary to optimize blockchain protocols, improve transaction speeds, reduce energy consumption, and enhance scalability. Ensuring the scalability and sustainability of blockchain systems will enable their effective use in combating corruption on a large scale.

Energy and Sustainability

- **Decentralized energy grids and peer-to-peer energy trading**

The global energy area is undergoing a profound transformation, driven by the need for sustainability, decentralization, and renewable energy sources. Traditional centralized energy systems face challenges related to inefficiency, lack of transparency, and limited consumer participation. However, the emergence of blockchain technology offers promising solutions, enabling the development of decentralized energy grids and facilitating peer-to-peer energy trading.

Traditional energy systems are centralized, controlled by a few entities, and predominantly rely on fossil fuels. This centralized structure limits consumer participation, inhibits the integration of renewable energy sources, and creates vulnerabilities in terms of reliability and resilience.

Transparency and trust are critical in energy transactions and pricing, yet the existing energy systems often lack sufficient transparency. Consumers have limited visibility into the sources and origins of the energy they consume, while centralized intermediaries dictate pricing and terms without adequate transparency, leading to potential issues of fairness and trust.

Centralized energy grids suffer from inefficiencies, such as transmission losses and grid constraints. These inefficiencies result in wasted energy and limit the potential for integrating distributed renewable energy sources into the grid, hampering efforts towards a cleaner and more sustainable energy future.

Blockchain technology enables peer-to-peer energy trading, allowing individuals and businesses to directly exchange energy without intermediaries. By utilizing smart contracts, energy producers can sell surplus energy to nearby consumers, creating a decentralized marketplace that promotes local energy generation, consumption, and self-sufficiency. Peer-to-peer energy trading empowers consumers, encourages renewable energy adoption, and promotes a more decentralized and resilient energy system.

Blockchain facilitates the development of decentralized energy grids by integrating renewable energy sources, energy storage systems, and demand response mechanisms. Through blockchain-based energy management systems, energy generation and consumption can be optimized in real-time, enhancing grid reliability, efficiency, and resilience. Decentralized energy grids enable a more flexible and sustainable energy system, where energy flows are managed in a distributed and efficient manner.

Blockchain's transparency and immutability ensure that energy transactions are recorded securely and transparently. This transparency enables consumers to track the origin of their energy, ensuring they are using renewable sources and promoting sustainability. It also fosters trust and eliminates the need for centralized intermediaries in energy transactions, reducing costs and enhancing the efficiency of the energy market.

Blockchain technology facilitates the formation of localized energy communities, where participants can produce, consume, and trade energy within a specific geographical area. Participants can collaborate to optimize energy usage, share excess energy, and reduce dependence on centralized energy sources. Localized energy communities empower individuals, promote energy self-sufficiency, and create resilient and sustainable local energy systems.

Blockchain streamlines the tracking and trading of RECs or Renewable Energy Certificates. This represent the environmental attributes of renewable energy generation and can be tokenized on the blockchain. This ensures transparency and facilitates reliable tracking and trading of renewable energy credits, promoting the development and adoption of renewable energy sources. REC tracking on the blockchain enhances accountability and creates a market for renewable energy attributes, incentivizing the growth of renewable energy projects.

Blockchain-enabled microgrids allow communities to create localized energy systems that can operate independently or interconnect with the main grid. These microgrids utilize blockchain technology to enable secure and efficient peer-to-peer energy sharing, fostering energy resilience and promoting community self-sufficiency. Energy sharing platforms based on blockchain facilitate the seamless exchange of energy between prosumers, reducing energy waste, promoting renewable energy integration, and empowering communities to actively participate in the energy transition.

The integration of blockchain technology in decentralized energy grids and peer-to-peer energy trading requires the development of supportive regulatory frameworks. Governments must adapt existing regulations to accommodate blockchain solutions and promote interoperability among different blockchain platforms to ensure seamless integration. Clear and forward-thinking regulatory frameworks are essential to facilitate the growth of decentralized energy systems.

Scalability is a critical challenge when applying blockchain technology to energy systems. The high transaction volumes and real-time requirements of energy grids necessitate efficient consensus mechanisms and scalable blockchain solutions. Integration with existing energy infrastructure and systems also requires careful planning and coordination to guarantee compatibility and optimal functioning. Continued research and development are essential to address scalability challenges and optimize the integration of blockchain in energy systems.

The success of decentralized energy grids and peer-to-peer energy trading relies on consumer awareness, participation, and adoption. Education campaigns, incentives, and user-friendly interfaces are necessary to empower consumers to actively engage in energy management, understand the benefits of decentralized systems, and make informed decisions. Consumer-centric approaches, clear communication, and accessible information are key to driving consumer participation in the transition towards decentralized energy grids.

As energy systems involve sensitive consumer data, privacy and security considerations are paramount. Blockchain systems must comply with data protection regulations and implement robust security measures to safeguard personal information and ensure the integrity of energy transactions. Privacy-enhancing technologies and encryption techniques can be integrated into blockchain-based energy systems to protect consumer data while maintaining the transparency and efficiency of the energy market.

- **Carbon credit markets and sustainable supply chains**

As the urgency to address climate change and promote sustainability grows, carbon credit markets and sustainable supply chains have emerged as crucial tools for reducing greenhouse gas emissions and fostering responsible business practices. However, these domains face challenges such as lack of transparency, limited trust, and inefficient tracking of carbon emissions.

Carbon credit markets and sustainable supply chains encounter several obstacles that hinder their effectiveness and credibility:

Transparency is a crucial factor for ensuring the integrity of carbon credits and sustainability claims. However, current systems often lack transparency, making it challenging for stakeholders to verify the authenticity and credibility of carbon credits and sustainable practices. This lack of transparency creates a trust deficit among participants in these markets.

Tracking and verifying carbon emissions and sustainability practices are complex and time-consuming processes. Existing systems rely heavily on manual documentation and auditing, leading to inefficiencies and delays. This lack of efficiency hampers the ability to accurately track and verify carbon credits or sustainable practices throughout the supply chain.

Accessibility and traceability of information are vital for ensuring accountability and promoting responsible practices. However, carbon credit markets and sustainable supply chains often struggle with limited access to relevant data, hindering stakeholders from making informed decisions, assessing the impact of their actions, and verifying the validity of carbon credits or sustainability claims.

Blockchain technology can bring transparency and accountability to carbon credit markets. By recording carbon credit transactions on a distributed ledger, blockchain ensures transparency and traceability, enabling stakeholders to verify the origin, ownership, and transfer of carbon credits. This transparency fosters trust and builds a more reliable market.

Blockchain's immutability ensures the integrity of carbon credit records. Once recorded on the blockchain, carbon credit transactions cannot be altered or tampered with retroactively. This feature provides an auditable trail, making it easier to verify the legitimacy of carbon credits and reducing the risk of fraudulent or double-counted credits.

Smart contracts, self-executing agreements that run on the blockchain, can automate compliance with carbon credit standards and regulations. These contracts automatically trigger the issuance, transfer, and retirement of carbon credits when predefined conditions are met. Smart contracts reduce administrative burdens, improve efficiency, and enhance compliance with carbon credit market rules.

Blockchain technology enables the development of decentralized carbon credit platforms where buyers and sellers can transact directly, eliminating the need for intermediaries. These platforms facilitate transparent and secure trading of carbon credits, reducing transaction costs and increasing market accessibility for both large and small players.

Blockchain can streamline the verification and certification process of carbon credits by providing an immutable record of emissions data and sustainability practices. By integrating Internet of Things (IoT) devices and sensors, emissions data can be reliably collected, recorded on the blockchain, and audited by third-party verifiers. This streamlined verification process enhances the credibility of carbon credits and ensures their integrity.

Blockchain can facilitate carbon offsetting and project financing by tokenizing carbon credits as digital assets. These tokens can be easily traded, allowing individuals and organizations to support carbon reduction projects and participate in carbon offsetting initiatives. Blockchain's transparency and traceability enable stakeholders to monitor the progress and impact of carbon reduction projects, enhancing accountability and investor confidence.

Blockchain enables end-to-end traceability in sustainable supply chains by recording each transaction and movement of goods on the blockchain. This transparent and immutable record allows consumers and stakeholders to track the entire lifecycle of products, ensuring the authenticity of sustainability claims and reducing the risk of greenwashing.

Blockchain can verify sustainability claims by storing relevant information, such as certifications, audits, and environmental impact data, on the blockchain. This data can be securely shared with stakeholders, allowing for transparent verification of sustainable practices and promoting trust throughout the supply chain.

Blockchain-based platforms can facilitate supplier management and compliance in sustainable supply chains. By recording supplier information, certifications, and compliance records on the blockchain, stakeholders can easily verify the sustainability credentials of their suppliers. Blockchain can also streamline supplier audits, simplifying the verification process and reducing administrative burdens.

To fully realize the capacity of blockchain in carbon credit markets and sustainable supply chains, standardization and interoperability are crucial. Collaborative efforts among industry players, regulatory bodies, and technology providers are needed to establish common protocols and data formats, ensuring seamless integration and compatibility across different blockchain platforms.

As carbon credit markets and sustainable supply chains involve sensitive data, privacy and security considerations must be addressed. Blockchain systems should incorporate robust privacy mechanisms and encryption techniques to protect confidential information while maintaining transparency and traceability. Adherence with data protection regulations is crucial to build trust and ensure responsible data handling practices.

Scalability and energy consumption are ongoing challenges that need to be addressed for widespread adoption of blockchain technology. Solutions such as off-chain scaling techniques and energy-efficient consensus algorithms can mitigate these concerns, making blockchain more sustainable and scalable.

- **Renewable energy certification and tracking**

The global effort towards renewable energy sources has created a need for robust certification and tracking systems to guarantee the integrity and transparency of renewable energy generation. However, traditional approaches in renewable energy certification and tracking face challenges such as lack of trust, limited transparency, and inefficiencies in verifying renewable energy attributes.

One of the key difficulties in renewable energy certification is the lack of transparency, making it challenging to validate the authenticity and accuracy of renewable energy attributes. This lack of transparency erodes trust among stakeholders and hampers the growth of renewable energy markets.

The verification and tracking of renewable energy attributes often involve manual and time-consuming processes. Traditional methods rely on paper-based documentation and auditing, leading to inefficiencies, delays, and potential errors in tracking renewable energy certificates.

Existing renewable energy certification systems struggle with limited accessibility and interoperability. This lack of standardized platforms and data formats hampers the efficient sharing and integration of renewable energy data across different stakeholders and market participants.

Blockchain technology provides a decentralized and transparent framework for renewable energy certification. By recording renewable energy generation data on a distributed ledger, blockchain ensures transparency and traceability, allowing stakeholders to validate the authenticity and provenance of renewable energy attributes. This transparency fosters trust and builds a more reliable market for renewable energy certificates.

One of the key features of blockchain is its immutability, which ensures the integrity of renewable energy certificates. Once recorded on the blockchain, data related to renewable energy generation cannot be altered or tampered with retroactively. This feature provides an auditable trail, making it easier to verify the legitimacy of renewable energy certificates and reducing the risk of fraudulent claims.

Smart contracts, self-executing agreements that run on the blockchain, can automate compliance with renewable energy standards and regulations. These contracts automatically trigger the issuance, transfer, and retirement of renewable energy certificates when predefined conditions are met. Smart contracts streamline administrative processes, improve efficiency, and enhance compliance with renewable energy market rules.

Blockchain technology can revolutionize the tracking and trading of RECs or Renewable Energy Certificates. This represent the environmental attributes of renewable energy generation and can be tokenized on the blockchain. This enables transparent and reliable tracking and trading of renewable energy credits, ensuring that each REC corresponds to a specific unit of renewable energy generated.

Blockchain-based decentralized marketplaces enable direct trading of renewable energy attributes, bypassing intermediaries. These platforms allow renewable energy producers to sell their energy attributes, such as carbon offsets or renewable energy certificates, directly to buyers, promoting efficiency, reducing transaction costs, and promoting the growth of renewable energy markets.

Blockchain facilitates peer-to-peer energy trading, allowing individuals and businesses to directly exchange renewable energy. By utilizing smart contracts, energy producers can sell excess renewable energy to nearby consumers, creating a decentralized marketplace that promotes local energy generation, consumption, and self-sufficiency.

The integration of blockchain technology in renewable energy certification requires supportive regulatory frameworks and standardization efforts. Governments and regulatory bodies must adapt existing regulations to accommodate blockchain solutions and promote interoperability among different blockchain platforms. Standardization ensures seamless integration and compatibility across renewable energy markets.

Scalability and energy consumption are important considerations in blockchain implementations. As renewable energy markets grow, blockchain systems need to handle increased transaction volumes efficiently. Energy-efficient consensus mechanisms and off-chain scaling solutions can mitigate scalability challenges and reduce the energy consumption associated with blockchain networks.

As renewable energy certification involves sensitive data, privacy and security considerations are paramount. Blockchain systems should comply with data protection regulations and implement robust security measures to safeguard personal information and ensure the integrity of renewable energy certificate transactions.

CHAPTER III

Challenges and
Limitations of Blockchain

Scalability and transaction throughput

Blockchain technology has garnered significant attention and adoption across various industries due to its decentralized, transparent, and immutable nature. However, scalability and transaction throughput have remained persistent challenges for blockchain networks, hindering their widespread use and applicability. As the demand for blockchain-based applications continues to grow, addressing these challenges becomes crucial. This section explores the concepts of scalability and transaction throughput in blockchain technology, examines the underlying issues, and discusses potential solutions to overcome these limitations.

A blockchain network's scalability refers to its ability to handle a growing volume of transactions or users without compromising effectiveness and performance. It is essential in deciding whether blockchain technology can be applied in the real world and is viable. As blockchain networks become more widely adopted, the need for scalable solutions becomes increasingly apparent.

Blockchain networks, such as Bitcoin and Ethereum, face scalability challenges due to their consensus mechanisms and data storage models. The inherent design of these networks limits the number of transactions that can be processed within a given time frame, leading to slower transaction speeds, higher fees, and network congestion.

Different consensus mechanisms, such as Proof of Work (PoW) and Proof of Stake (PoS), have varying impacts on scalability. PoW, while secure, requires extensive computational resources, limiting the transaction throughput. PoS, on the other hand, offers higher scalability potential by reducing resource requirements but introduces new challenges.

The design of the blockchain network, including block size and block time, affects scalability. Larger block sizes can accommodate more transactions per block but require increased storage capacity and processing power. Smaller block sizes may improve decentralization but limit the number of transactions that can be included in each block.

The ability of different blockchain networks to communicate and perform cross-chain transactions is critical for scalability. Interoperability protocols, such as atomic swaps and sidechains, enable seamless transfer of assets and also data between different blockchain networks, enhancing scalability and expanding the potential use cases.

Sharding entails dividing the blockchain network into smaller subsets called shards, each capable of processing its transactions. This approach improves scalability by parallelizing transaction processing and reducing the burden on individual nodes. However, implementing sharding requires careful coordination and synchronization to maintain network security and consistency.

Layer 2 scaling solutions, like payment channels (e.g., Lightning Network) and state channels, enable off-chain transactions and reduce the load on the main blockchain. By conducting transactions off-chain and settling them periodically on the main blockchain, these solutions significantly improve scalability and reduce transaction costs.

New consensus algorithms are being developed to improve scalability without compromising security. For instance, delegated Proof of Stake (DPoS) and Byzantine Fault Tolerance (BFT) consensus algorithms aim to increase transaction throughput by reducing the number of participants involved in the consensus process.

Transaction throughput is the number of transactions a blockchain network are able to process within a given time frame. High transaction throughput is essential for applications requiring fast and efficient transaction processing, such as payment systems and supply chain management.

The limited transaction throughput of existing blockchain networks hinders their scalability and mass adoption. The confirmation time for transactions can be lengthy, resulting in delays and increased costs, making blockchain less suitable for high-frequency transaction environments.

Off-chain transactions, facilitated by Layer 2 scaling solutions, allow parties to conduct transactions without directly involving the main blockchain. By reducing the number of on-chain transactions, transaction throughput can be significantly increased, enabling faster and more cost-effective transactions.

Efficient data structures, such as Merkle trees and compressed transaction formats, can enhance transaction throughput by reducing the size of transactions and optimizing data storage. These optimizations allow more transactions to be included in a block, improving the overall transaction processing speed.

Advancements in hardware, such as faster processors and improved network infrastructure, can enhance transaction throughput. Optimizing network protocols, including peer-to-peer communication and data propagation, can also reduce latency and increase transaction processing speed.

Energy consumption and environmental concerns

Blockchain technology has acquired significant attention and adoption across various industries for its decentralized, transparent, and secure nature. However, as the popularity of blockchain grows, so does the concern over its energy consumption and environmental impact. This section explores the energy consumption of blockchain technology, its environmental implications, and potential strategies to mitigate its environmental footprint.

Blockchain technology, particularly in cryptocurrencies like Bitcoin and Ethereum, is known for its energy-intensive nature. The primary driver of energy consumption in blockchain is the Proof of Work consensus mechanism, which demands miners to solve complex mathematical puzzles to validate transactions and secure the network. The computational power required for this process translates into significant energy consumption.

The energy consumption of blockchain is further influenced by scalability challenges and the data storage requirements of the technology. Blockchain scalability issues, such as limited transaction throughput and increasing block sizes, contribute to higher energy consumption. As the network grows, more computational power and energy are required to process and validate transactions, resulting in increased electricity consumption. Additionally, the distributed nature of blockchain requires data replication across multiple nodes, leading to redundant energy usage for data storage and synchronization.

The energy consumption of blockchain technology has direct environmental implications, primarily through the generation of greenhouse gas emissions and the production of electronic waste.

Blockchain networks' high energy requirements, frequently powered by electricity produced from fossil fuels, contribute to the release of greenhouse gases, mostly carbon dioxide. The carbon footprint of blockchain networks is a growing concern as it exacerbates climate change and undermines efforts to transition to a low-carbon economy. As the acceptance of blockchain continues to rise, so does its environmental impact.

Blockchain mining activities, particularly in PoW blockchains, involve the use of specialized hardware that requires frequent upgrades to maintain competitiveness. This rapid obsolescence of mining equipment contributes to electronic waste generation, as outdated hardware becomes obsolete and is often discarded. The disposal of electronic waste poses environmental challenges, including resource depletion and the proper management of hazardous materials.

Addressing the energy consumption as well as environmental impact of blockchain technology requires a multi-faceted approach. Several strategies can be employed to mitigate these concerns.

Exploring alternative consensus mechanisms, such as Proof of Stake (PoS) and also Delegated Proof of Stake (DPoS), can significantly reduce the energy consumption of blockchain networks. Unlike PoW, these consensus mechanisms do not require miners to solve complex puzzles but instead assign block validation rights based on the participants' stake in the network. This shift reduces the computational power and energy required for consensus, making the network more energy-efficient.

Optimizing blockchain protocols can contribute to energy efficiency. Techniques such as sharding, where the network is divided into smaller subsets, and off-chain transactions can increase scalability and reduce energy consumption. By conducting transactions off-chain and settling them periodically on the main blockchain, these solutions significantly improve scalability and reduce transaction costs.

Promoting the utilization of renewable energy sources for blockchain mining operations can help mitigate the environmental impact. By powering blockchain networks with clean energy, the carbon footprint can be reduced, and the transition to a sustainable energy future can be accelerated. Collaborating with renewable energy providers and investing in renewable energy infrastructure can ensure a greener energy supply for blockchain operations.

Compensating for the carbon emissions associated with blockchain operations through carbon offset initiatives can contribute to environmental sustainability. Supporting renewable energy projects, reforestation efforts, or investing in carbon credits can help offset the environmental impact of blockchain technology. This approach aligns with the concept of "carbon neutrality" by balancing the emissions produced with equivalent reductions or removals of greenhouse gases elsewhere.

Addressing the energy consumption as well as environmental impact of blockchain technology requires collaboration among stakeholders, including researchers, industry players, and regulatory bodies. The following initiatives can facilitate the development and adoption of sustainable blockchain solutions:

Continued research and development efforts are essential to identify and implement energy-efficient solutions for blockchain technology. Collaboration between academia, industry players, and governments can drive innovation and promote the development of sustainable blockchain solutions. Research can focus on improving consensus mechanisms, optimizing protocols, and developing more energy-efficient mining hardware.

Regulatory frameworks that incentivize energy-efficient blockchain practices and encourage the use of renewable energy can play a crucial role in lessening the environmental impact. Establishing guidelines and standards for energy consumption and carbon emissions can promote responsible blockchain operations. Regulatory bodies can also encourage transparency and disclosure of environmental metrics by blockchain projects, enabling stakeholders to make informed decisions.

Collaborative initiatives among blockchain projects, mining companies, and energy providers can facilitate the adoption of renewable energy sources and promote responsible energy consumption practices. Sharing best practices, fostering transparency, and setting industry-wide sustainability goals can contribute to a greener blockchain ecosystem. Partnerships between blockchain projects and renewable energy providers can drive the development of dedicated renewable energy facilities to power blockchain operations.

Regulatory and legal hurdles

Blockchain technology has appeared as a transformative force across various industries, offering decentralized and transparent solutions for various applications. However, as the adoption of blockchain expands, regulatory and legal hurdles have become significant challenges. This section will explore the regulatory and legal landscape surrounding blockchain technology, identifies key hurdles, and discusses potential strategies to address these obstacles.

Blockchain technology operates within a complex and evolving regulatory landscape, varying across jurisdictions worldwide. The regulatory approaches to blockchain range from supportive and progressive to cautious and restrictive. Governments and regulatory bodies aim to strike a balance between promoting innovation and protecting public interest by developing appropriate regulatory frameworks for blockchain technology.

Different countries have adopted diverse approaches to regulating blockchain technology. Some nations have embraced blockchain, providing a conducive environment for innovation, while others have taken a cautious approach, introducing stringent regulations to mitigate potential risks associated with the technology.

The objectives of blockchain regulation often revolve around consumer protection, anti-money laundering (AML) and counter-terrorism financing (CTF) measures, investor safeguards, privacy, data protection, and ensuring the integrity of financial markets. Balancing innovation and these regulatory objectives is a key challenge in the development of appropriate regulatory frameworks.

The rapidly evolving nature of blockchain technology has led to regulatory uncertainty and a lack of clarity. Policymakers as well as regulators struggle to keep pace with technological advancements, resulting in inconsistent or ambiguous regulations that create uncertainty for businesses and hinder innovation. Clear and well-defined regulations are essential to provide a stable and predictable environment for blockchain development and adoption.

Determining the classification of blockchain-based assets, such as cryptocurrencies and utility tokens, poses a challenge. Different regulatory classifications may result in regulatory arbitrage, where businesses relocate to jurisdictions with more favorable regulatory environments, potentially undermining the effectiveness of regulations. Harmonizing the classification of blockchain assets is crucial to ensure consistent and coherent regulatory frameworks globally.

The decentralized nature of blockchain technology presents challenges in regulating cross-border transactions. Determining jurisdiction and enforcing regulations becomes complex when multiple parties and transactions span different jurisdictions. Harmonizing regulations across borders is crucial to enable seamless cross-border transactions while addressing regulatory concerns.

The General Data Protection Regulation of the European Union and other data privacy laws are in contradiction with the transparent and immutable characteristics of the blockchain. In order to comply with data protection rules and utilize the advantages of blockchain technology, finding a balance between openness as well as privacy is a crucial task. Innovative approaches, such as zero-knowledge proofs and privacy-focused blockchain solutions, can help address these concerns.

Regulatory sandboxes provide a controlled environment for blockchain startups and businesses to test innovative solutions under regulatory supervision. These sandboxes allow regulators to observe and understand blockchain technology while enabling businesses to experiment with compliant solutions, fostering innovation within a regulated framework. Regulatory sandboxes facilitate collaboration between regulators and industry participants to identify potential risks, assess regulatory impacts, and develop appropriate regulations.

Engaging in dialogue and collaboration between blockchain industry participants and regulators is crucial for developing effective and balanced regulations. Regular consultations, workshops, and industry feedback can help policymakers gain insights into blockchain technology and its potential impact, leading to informed and pragmatic regulations. Open communication channels between regulators and industry stakeholders can facilitate a better understanding of technological advancements and regulatory requirements.

Addressing regulatory challenges requires interdisciplinary collaboration involving legal experts, technologists, policymakers, and industry stakeholders. This collaboration can bridge the gap between technological innovations and regulatory frameworks, fostering an understanding of the potential risks and rewards of blockchain technology. Interdisciplinary teams can provide comprehensive insights into the legal, technical, and economic aspects of blockchain, enabling regulators to develop informed regulations.

Cooperation among countries to develop common regulatory frameworks and standards can promote regulatory clarity and consistency in the global blockchain ecosystem. International organizations as well as regulatory bodies, such as the International Organization for Standardization (ISO), can play a key role in facilitating dialogue, information sharing, and the development of interoperable regulatory frameworks. Standardization efforts can enhance regulatory harmonization, reduce regulatory arbitrage, and foster global collaboration in blockchain technology.

Implementing robust Know Your Customer (KYC) and Anti-Money Laundering (AML) procedures can help mitigate risks associated with blockchain technology, ensuring compliance with regulatory requirements and preventing illicit activities. The integration of blockchain-based identity solutions and the use of advanced cryptographic techniques can enhance identity verification and transaction monitoring in a secure and privacy-preserving manner.

Clarifying the legal status and enforceability of smart contracts is crucial for widespread adoption. Establishing frameworks that recognize the legal validity of smart contracts can provide certainty and facilitate their use in various industries, including finance, supply chain, and legal sectors. Governments can enact legislation that recognizes the unique features and characteristics of smart contracts while ensuring they align with existing legal frameworks.

Intellectual property challenges arise in blockchain technology due to the open-source characteristic of many blockchain projects. Developing mechanisms to protect intellectual property rights while fostering innovation and collaboration is essential. Governments and industry organizations can establish frameworks and incentives that encourage the development and protection of intellectual property within the blockchain ecosystem.

Privacy and data protection issues

Blockchain technology has acquired significant attention for its ability to revolutionize industries by providing transparency, immutability, and security. However, the distributed and transparent nature of blockchain raises concerns regarding privacy and data protection. This section explores the privacy and data protection challenges in blockchain technology, examines the impact on individuals and organizations, and discusses potential strategies to address these issues while harnessing the benefits of blockchain.

Privacy is the right of individuals to control the collection, use, and disclosure of their personal information. Blockchain's transparent nature challenges traditional notions of privacy, as transaction data recorded on the blockchain is visible to all participants. This transparency raises concerns regarding the exposure of sensitive personal information.

Data protection involves safeguarding personal data from unauthorized access, use, and disclosure. Blockchain's immutability and decentralized nature present unique challenges to data protection. Once data is recorded on the blockchain, it becomes virtually impossible to alter or erase, potentially conflicting with the "right to be forgotten" principle.

While blockchain uses pseudonymous addresses to protect the identities of participants, the transparent nature of blockchain allows for the potential linkage of transactions to real-world identities. This can compromise privacy, as transactions conducted on the blockchain can be traced back to specific individuals.

Public blockchains, such as Ethereum and Bitcoin, offer limited privacy protections as all transaction details are publicly accessible. In contrast, private blockchains provide more control over privacy but sacrifice the transparency and trust provided by public blockchains.

Smart contracts, self-executing agreements recorded on the blockchain, can pose privacy risks when personal or sensitive information is embedded within them. The immutability of the blockchain means that once information is recorded in a smart contract, it cannot be easily modified or deleted.

Blockchain's decentralized nature and the potential for data to reside in multiple jurisdictions raise challenges in complying with diverse data protection laws across different regions. Ensuring compliance with regulations, like the European Union's General Data Protection Regulation (GDPR), becomes complex when data is distributed across multiple nodes.

Integrating enhanced privacy measures into blockchain protocols can help protect personal data while maintaining transparency. Techniques such as zero-knowledge proofs, ring signatures, and homomorphic encryption can enable privacy-preserving transactions on the blockchain, ensuring the confidentiality of sensitive information.

Implementing robust identity management systems can help maintain pseudonymity on the blockchain. By separating real-world identities from blockchain addresses, individuals can participate in transactions while minimizing the risk of identity exposure.

Adopting privacy by design principles involves integrating privacy considerations from the early stages of blockchain development. Privacy-enhancing technologies, privacy impact assessments, and consent management mechanisms can be implemented to embed privacy as a fundamental component of blockchain systems.

Permissioned blockchains provide a balance between privacy and transparency by limiting access to trusted participants. Consortium blockchains, where multiple organizations collaborate, can establish data protection agreements and privacy policies tailored to their specific needs, ensuring compliance with regulations.

Navigating diverse data protection regulations and cross-border data transfers require compliance with regional and international frameworks. Blockchain projects must assess and align their operations with relevant data protection laws, ensuring transparency and compliance with privacy requirements.

Collaboration between regulators, industry stakeholders, and privacy experts can help develop appropriate regulatory frameworks for blockchain technology. Dialogue and cooperation can foster the development of privacy-preserving solutions while addressing regulatory concerns and promoting innovation.

Raising awareness about privacy and data protection in the blockchain ecosystem is crucial. Educating users, developers, and organizations about best practices, legal obligations, and privacy risks can empower them to make informed decisions and adopt privacy-enhancing measures.

Transparency is a core benefit of blockchain technology, facilitating trust, auditability, and accountability. Balancing privacy with transparency requires careful consideration to ensure that personal information is protected while maintaining the integrity and security of the blockchain.

Blockchain can empower individuals by providing greater control over their personal data. Implementing consent management mechanisms and giving users the ability to manage their data and determine its disclosure on the blockchain can enhance privacy and data protection.

Privacy and data protection issues in blockchain require collaboration among stakeholders, including developers, regulators, privacy advocates, and end-users. Engaging in dialogue, sharing best practices, and adopting privacy-enhancing technologies collectively can drive responsible blockchain innovation while safeguarding privacy.

CHAPTER IV

Future Trends and Emerging Developments

Layer 2 solutions and blockchain interoperability

Blockchain technology has shown immense promise in revolutionizing industries with its decentralized and secure nature. However, scalability limitations and the lack of interoperability between different blockchain networks have hindered widespread adoption. This section delves into the concepts of Layer 2 solutions and blockchain interoperability, exploring their significance, challenges, and potential solutions for advancing scalability and connectivity in the blockchain ecosystem.

Blockchain technology's decentralized nature and consensus mechanisms pose challenges in achieving high transaction throughput and quick block confirmation times. To address these scalability issues, Layer 2 solutions have emerged as an approach to enable off-chain transactions while leveraging the security as well as decentralization of the underlying blockchain. These solutions build upon existing blockchain networks, providing additional layers of infrastructure that can handle a large number of transactions without burdening the main blockchain.

There are many kinds of Layer 2 solutions that aim to address scalability challenges while maintaining the integrity of the blockchain ecosystem. One such solution is payment channels, such as the Lightning Network for Bitcoin. Payment channels facilitate off-chain transactions between participants, allowing multiple transactions to be conducted without each one needing to be recorded on the blockchain. This reduces congestion and lowers transaction costs, enabling faster and more cost-effective payments.

Another type of Layer 2 solution is sidechains, which are separate blockchain networks that are interoperable with the main chain. Sidechains enable the transfer of assets between the main chain and sidechain, enabling faster and more efficient processing of transactions specific to a particular use case. State channels are also an important Layer 2 solution that enables off-chain execution of smart contracts. Participants can interact and update the contract's state without every interaction being recorded on the main blockchain. This approach significantly reduces transaction costs and improves scalability for applications that require frequent and rapid updates.

Layer 2 solutions offer several advantages that address scalability challenges and enhance the usability of blockchain technology. Firstly, these solutions provide scalability by significantly increasing transaction throughput, reducing congestion, and improving user experience. They enable blockchain networks to handle a larger volume of transactions, making them more suitable for mainstream adoption.

Secondly, Layer 2 solutions offer cost efficiency by reducing transaction fees. Off-chain transactions typically incur lower fees and allow for micropayments, making blockchain technology more accessible and economically viable for various use cases. Thirdly, these solutions enhance transaction speed by processing transactions off-chain. This near-instantaneous transaction confirmation improves the efficiency of blockchain applications, enabling real-time interactions and faster settlement times.

Additionally, Layer 2 solutions can enhance privacy by conducting transactions off-chain, reducing the visibility of transaction details to the broader network. However, Layer 2 solutions also come with their own set of challenges. Security is a critical consideration, as the security of Layer 2 solutions heavily relies on the underlying blockchain's security. It is essential to ensure that the protocols and mechanisms used in Layer 2 solutions do not compromise the overall security of the ecosystem.

Interoperability between different Layer 2 solutions and blockchain networks is another challenge. Seamless communication and transfer of assets across different chains require standardized protocols and frameworks to ensure compatibility and interoperability.

Furthermore, adoption and standardization play significant roles in the success of Layer 2 solutions. The integration of these solutions into existing blockchain networks and their acceptance by developers and users are crucial for their widespread adoption. Standardization efforts are necessary to ensure compatibility and interoperability between different Layer 2 solutions.

Interoperability refers to the capacity of different blockchain networks to communicate, share data, and transfer assets seamlessly. Achieving interoperability is crucial for realizing the full potential of blockchain technology, enabling cross-chain transactions, and fostering collaboration among disparate networks. Achieving interoperability presents various challenges. Technical compatibility is a significant hurdle, as different blockchains employ varying consensus mechanisms, smart contract languages, and data structures. Establishing seamless interoperability requires developing standardized communication protocols that facilitate secure and efficient communication between different blockchains.

Governance and coordination among multiple stakeholders are also critical challenges in achieving blockchain interoperability. Establishing governance models and standards that facilitate interoperability is a complex task, as it requires coordination among developers, miners, validators, and network participants. Security and trust are additional concerns when it comes to interoperability. Establishing mechanisms to ensure the integrity of cross-chain transactions, prevent double-spending, and maintain data consistency is essential.

Firstly, cross-chain communication protocols provide standardized communication protocols that enable secure and efficient communication between different blockchains. These protocols facilitate interoperability by enabling the transfer of assets and data across different chains. Secondly, atomic swaps allow for direct peer-to-peer exchanges of assets across different blockchains without relying on intermediaries. This approach ensures trustless and decentralized asset transfers.

Lastly, bridge and wrapper solutions enable the transfer of assets between different blockchains by locking assets in one chain and issuing wrapped tokens representing the value on another chain. These solutions provide compatibility and liquidity across disparate networks.

The future of Layer 2 solutions and blockchain interoperability lies in continued research, innovation, and collaboration. Advancing the state of the art in Layer 2 solutions and interoperability protocols requires the involvement of academic institutions, industry research labs, and blockchain communities. Standardization efforts, collaborative initiatives, and industry-wide cooperation are vital for achieving seamless interoperability. Developing common protocols, data formats, and governance models can foster compatibility and create a thriving ecosystem of interconnected blockchains.

Additionally, layer 2 solutions can play a pivotal role in achieving blockchain interoperability. By utilizing sidechains, state channels, or payment channels, Layer 2 solutions can enable cross-chain transactions, asset transfers, and data sharing while preserving the security and decentralization of the underlying blockchains.

Integration with Internet of Things (IoT) devices

The propagation of Internet of Things or IoT devices has transformed the way we interact with our surroundings, enabling seamless connectivity and data exchange. However, the decentralized and vulnerable nature of IoT ecosystems raises concerns about data integrity, security, and trust. This section explores the integration of blockchain technology with IoT devices, examining the potential benefits, challenges, and applications of this convergence, and discussing strategies to enhance security and trust in the interconnected world.

IoT devices encompass a wide range of interconnected objects, such as sensors, wearables, appliances, and industrial equipment, that collect and exchange data. These devices enable real-time monitoring, automation, and data-driven decision-making across various sectors, including healthcare, manufacturing, transportation, and smart cities.

IoT networks face inherent vulnerabilities due to the massive number of devices, diverse communication protocols, and centralized points of failure. These vulnerabilities expose data to security breaches, unauthorized access, and tampering, compromising the privacy and integrity of IoT-generated data.

Blockchain's decentralized and immutable nature can enhance security and data integrity in IoT ecosystems. By storing data in a tamper-resistant and transparent manner, blockchain ensures the integrity and traceability of IoT-generated data, reducing the risk of data manipulation and unauthorized access.

Blockchain enables secure peer-to-peer communication and data exchange among IoT devices, eliminating the need for intermediaries and fostering trust in data transactions. Smart contracts, self-executing agreements kept on the blockchain, can automate interactions between IoT devices based on predefined conditions, enhancing transparency and efficiency.

Blockchain-based identity management and encryption mechanisms can address privacy concerns in IoT networks. Users can have control over their data by granting access permissions and selectively sharing data with authorized entities, ensuring privacy while enabling data sharing for valuable insights and services.

The integration of blockchain and IoT poses challenges in terms of scalability and performance. The high volume of transactions created by IoT devices may strain the capacity of traditional blockchain networks. Innovative approaches, such as sharding, off-chain processing, and Layer 2 solutions, are being explored to address these scalability concerns.

IoT devices often operate on different communication protocols and standards, hindering seamless integration with blockchain networks. Achieving interoperability between diverse IoT devices and blockchain platforms requires the development of standardized protocols and frameworks.

Many IoT devices have limited computational power, storage capacity, and energy resources. Optimizing blockchain protocols and designing lightweight consensus mechanisms tailored to resource-constrained devices are essential for efficient and sustainable integration.

Blockchain-IoT integration can revolutionize supply chain management by providing end-to-end visibility, traceability, and transparency. IoT sensors can track goods throughout the supply chain, recording data on the blockchain. This enables real-time monitoring, authentication, and verification of products, reducing counterfeiting, ensuring product quality, and optimizing logistics.

Blockchain-IoT integration can enhance the efficiency and security of smart cities. IoT devices can collect data on traffic, energy consumption, waste management, and public services, which can be securely stored and accessed on the blockchain. This enables decentralized decision-making, automated transactions, and the creation of trusted and efficient urban ecosystems.

Blockchain can empower patients by providing secure and decentralized storage of health records and enabling data sharing with healthcare providers. IoT wearable devices can generate real-time health data, which can be securely transmitted to the blockchain for analysis, diagnosis, and personalized healthcare services.

Selecting consensus mechanisms suitable for IoT devices, such as lightweight consensus algorithms, can optimize performance and reduce energy consumption. Data validation mechanisms, such as zero-knowledge proofs, can ensure the authenticity and integrity of IoT-generated data.

Implementing blockchain-based identity management systems can enhance security and privacy in IoT networks. Decentralized identity solutions enable secure device authentication, access control, and user privacy, ensuring that only authorized entities can interact with IoT devices.

Hybrid architectures that combine blockchain with off-chain storage and processing can optimize performance and scalability in IoT networks. Off-chain processing can handle computationally intensive tasks, while critical data and transactions are securely recorded on the blockchain.

The integration of blockchain with IoT devices holds immense potential for enhancing security, trust, and efficiency in a connected world. By leveraging blockchain's decentralized, transparent, and immutable nature, IoT ecosystems can benefit from enhanced data integrity, secure peer-to-peer communication, and trusted data exchange. However, addressing scalability, interoperability, and resource constraints remain critical challenges.

By developing scalable and optimized blockchain protocols, establishing interoperability standards, and adopting secure identity and access management mechanisms, the convergence of blockchain and IoT can unlock new possibilities across sectors, including supply chain management, smart cities, and healthcare. This integration has the power to reshape industries, empower individuals, and create a more secure and efficient interconnected world.

Artificial intelligence and machine learning in blockchain

The convergence of artificial intelligence (AI) as well as machine learning (ML) with blockchain technology has the potential to revolutionize industries, develop new opportunities, and shape the future of innovation. AI and ML have emerged as transformative technologies, capable of analyzing huge amounts of data, making predictions, and automating complex tasks. Meanwhile, blockchain offers a decentralized, transparent, and secure platform for recording and verifying transactions. This section explores the integration of AI/ML with blockchain, examining the synergies between the two, the challenges and considerations, and the implications for innovation and societal impact.

AI encompasses the simulation of human intelligence in machines, allowing them to perform tasks that usually require human cognitive abilities. ML, a subset of AI, focuses on algorithms as well as statistical models that allow machines to learn from data, make predictions, and improve performance over time. On the other hand, blockchain technology is a decentralized distributed ledger that stores and verifies transactions across multiple nodes, ensuring transparency, security, and immutability.

Blockchain provides a decentralized and transparent platform for data storage and sharing. This availability of reliable data is crucial for training AI/ML models, enabling more accurate predictions and insights. With blockchain acting as a trusted data source, AI/ML algorithms can leverage the immutability and integrity of the data recorded on the blockchain.

The cryptographic protocols and distributed nature of blockchain can enhance data privacy and security, addressing concerns that arise in AI/ML applications. By enabling secure and auditable data sharing, blockchain helps build trust and ensures data integrity in AI/ML systems. This integration can alleviate concerns related to data breaches, unauthorized access, and tampering.

Blockchain facilitates the development of decentralized AI/ML models by allowing multiple participants to contribute data and computational resources. This collaborative approach enhances model accuracy, fairness, and robustness while protecting individual data privacy. Decentralized models ensure that data is not concentrated in the hands of a single entity, promoting trust and transparency.

AI/ML algorithms can analyze data and automate the execution of smart contracts based on pre-established conditions. This integration can streamline complex contract processes, reduce human intervention, and enhance efficiency. Smart contracts powered by AI/ML algorithms can automatically verify conditions, trigger actions, and facilitate seamless interactions between parties, all while ensuring transparency and accuracy.

AI/ML algorithms can analyze transaction data recorded on the blockchain to detect anomalies, identify patterns, and predict fraudulent activities. By continuously monitoring and analyzing transactions, these algorithms can provide real-time fraud detection and risk management solutions. This integration enhances the security and trustworthiness of blockchain networks, particularly in financial and supply chain domains.

AI/ML techniques can process and analyze large volumes of data recorded on the blockchain, uncovering valuable insights and patterns that can inform decision-making, optimize processes, and drive innovation in various sectors. By combining AI/ML capabilities with the transparency and reliability of blockchain, organizations can gain an in-depth understanding of their operations, customer behavior, and market trends.

Integrating AI/ML with blockchain raises scalability challenges due to the computational as well as storage requirements of ML algorithms. Traditional blockchain networks may struggle to handle the processing power and storage demands of complex AI/ML models. Innovative solutions such as off-chain processing, sharding, and Layer 2 solutions are being explored to address these challenges and enable efficient integration.

While blockchain ensures data integrity, preserving privacy in AI/ML applications requires careful consideration. Balancing the transparency inherent in blockchain with the need to protect sensitive data poses challenges that necessitate privacy-preserving techniques and robust data governance frameworks. Ensuring compliance with data protection regulations while harnessing the benefits of AI/ML and blockchain integration is essential.

AI/ML models trained on blockchain data are susceptible to biases and ethical concerns. Training models on historical blockchain data may perpetuate biases present in the data, leading to biased decision-making. It is crucial to address issues such as algorithmic fairness, transparency, and accountability to ensure the responsible and unbiased use of AI/ML in blockchain systems. Continual monitoring and evaluation are necessary to identify and mitigate any unintended consequences.

Federated learning allows AI/ML models to be trained on decentralized data without compromising individual data privacy. The integration of federated learning with blockchain can facilitate collaborative model training while preserving privacy. By ensuring that sensitive data remains on local devices and only aggregated insights are shared on the blockchain, privacy concerns can be effectively addressed.

Combining blockchain's identity management capabilities with AI/ML can enable self-sovereign identity, where individuals have control over their data and can customize AI/ML models to suit their preferences and needs. This empowers individuals to share data selectively, maintain ownership of their digital identity, and enjoy personalized AI-driven services.

AI/ML techniques can analyze blockchain data to derive insights for governance decisions, such as consensus algorithm optimization, network scalability, and security enhancements. The integration of AI/ML-driven governance can contribute to the evolution and improvement of blockchain protocols, ensuring adaptability, efficiency, and sustainability.

Potential impact on emerging technologies

Emerging technologies are shaping the world we live in, with advancements in areas such as artificial intelligence (AI), Internet of Things (IoT), augmented reality (AR), and quantum computing presenting new possibilities and transforming various industries. Among these emerging technologies, blockchain has gained significant attention for its decentralized, transparent, and secure nature. This section explores the potential impact of blockchain on emerging technologies, examining the synergies, challenges, and opportunities that arise from their integration, and discussing the implications for innovation and societal progress.

Artificial Intelligence (AI) involves the simulation of human intelligence in machines, enabling them to learn, reason, and make decisions. It encompasses areas like machine learning, natural language processing, computer vision, and robotics.

The Internet of Things (IoT) refers to the network of interconnected objects and devices that collect and exchange data. These devices, including sensors, wearables, and smart appliances, enable seamless connectivity and data sharing.

Augmented Reality (AR) combines virtual elements with the real world, increasing our perception and interaction with the physical environment. It overlays digital information, such as graphics or data, onto real-world objects.

Quantum Computing leverages the concepts of quantum mechanics to perform computations at an exponential speed compared to classical computers. It has the potential to solve complex problems in fields like cryptography, optimization, and drug discovery.

Blockchain's decentralized and immutable nature enhances data security and trust, providing a foundation for emerging technologies. By securing data integrity, blockchain can enable secure transactions, privacy preservation, and trustworthy interactions in AI, IoT, AR, and quantum computing applications.

Blockchain's distributed ledger enables transparent and efficient data sharing, which can benefit AI algorithms by providing diverse and reliable datasets. Similarly, IoT devices can securely share data on the blockchain, creating new opportunities for data monetization and enabling AI-powered insights.

Blockchain's self-sovereign identity capabilities can enhance identity management in emerging technologies. It can provide secure and decentralized identity verification, facilitating seamless interactions and trust among AI systems, IoT devices, AR applications, and quantum computing networks.

Blockchain's transparent and tamper-proof nature can address the challenge of acquiring reliable and diverse datasets for AI training. Blockchain-powered data marketplaces can incentivize individuals to contribute data, ensuring a more representative and inclusive training process. Blockchain's transparent record-keeping capabilities can enhance the explainability and auditability of AI systems. By recording the decisions and data inputs on the blockchain, AI models can be audited, providing insights into the decision-making process and enabling accountability. Combining blockchain's decentralized nature with AI can enable the development of distributed and collaborative AI models. This approach facilitates secure and privacy-preserving collaborations, enabling multiple parties to contribute data and computing resources while preserving data sovereignty.

Blockchain can enhance the integrity and security of IoT data by providing a transparent and tamper-proof record of device interactions and transactions. This ensures the reliability and trustworthiness of IoT-generated data, critical for applications such as smart cities, supply chain management, and healthcare. Blockchain can enable interoperability among different IoT devices, platforms, and networks. By establishing common protocols and smart contract standards, blockchain facilitates seamless communication, data exchange, and automation across diverse IoT ecosystems. Blockchain can revolutionize the energy sector by enabling peer-to-peer energy trading among IoT devices. This decentralized approach empowers energy producers and consumers, reduces reliance on centralized utilities, and promotes sustainable energy practices.

Blockchain can ensure the authenticity and ownership of digital assets in AR applications. By recording ownership and transaction history on the blockchain, creators can protect their intellectual property rights, prevent unauthorized replication, and enable secure peer-to-peer transactions. Blockchain-based platforms can facilitate decentralized content distribution in AR. This enables independent creators to distribute their content directly to users, eliminating intermediaries and providing more diverse and personalized AR experiences. Blockchain can revolutionize AR advertising by enabling transparent and user-controlled data sharing. Users can selectively share their data with advertisers, ensuring privacy while allowing for more personalized and targeted advertising experiences.

Blockchain can benefit from quantum-resistant cryptographic techniques. As quantum computers pose a potential threat to traditional encryption methods, integrating quantum-resistant algorithms into blockchain can safeguard the security and privacy of blockchain networks. Blockchain's distributed consensus algorithms can be applied to quantum networks, enabling secure and decentralized communication among quantum devices. This can enhance the reliability and efficiency of quantum computing networks and enable distributed quantum computing applications. Blockchain can leverage the computational power of quantum computers to solve complex optimization problems. By integrating quantum algorithms into blockchain networks, optimization tasks such as supply chain management, portfolio optimization, and logistics planning can be significantly improved.

The integration of blockchain with emerging technologies presents scalability challenges. Blockchain networks need to handle a massive volume of transactions and computational requirements of AI, IoT, AR, and quantum computing applications. Research and innovation are required to develop scalable solutions that can meet the requirements of these technologies.

Interoperability and standardization are crucial for the seamless integration of blockchain with emerging technologies. Establishing common protocols, data formats, and interoperability frameworks are necessary to enable smooth data exchange, communication, and collaboration across diverse platforms and ecosystems.

As emerging technologies gather more personal and sensitive data, privacy protection and ethical considerations become paramount. Blockchain's transparency must be balanced with privacy-preserving techniques to ensure the responsible and ethical use of data in AI, IoT, AR, and quantum computing applications.

The integration of blockchain with emerging technologies requires collaborative research and innovation efforts. Academic institutions, industry leaders, and government agencies need to foster interdisciplinary collaboration to explore the full potential of these technologies and address the challenges that arise.

As blockchain and emerging technologies continue to evolve, regulatory and policy frameworks must keep pace. Governments and regulatory bodies need to establish guidelines and standards that promote innovation, ensure data privacy and security, and mitigate risks associated with these technologies.

The ethical adoption and responsible innovation of blockchain and emerging technologies should be a priority. Transparency, accountability, and inclusivity should be at the forefront of development and deployment to avoid unintended consequences and ensure equitable access to the benefits of these technologies.

The integration of blockchain with emerging technologies presents exciting opportunities to transform industries, drive innovation, and improve societal outcomes. By leveraging blockchain's decentralization, transparency, and security, AI, IoT, AR, and quantum computing can achieve new levels of efficiency, privacy, and reliability. However, addressing scalability, interoperability, privacy, and ethical considerations is crucial for realizing the full potential of these integrations. With continued research, collaboration, and responsible innovation, the combined impact of blockchain and emerging technologies can reshape the future, paving the way for a more connected, secure, and inclusive digital world.

CHAPTER V

Beyond Industries:
Social and Humanitarian Applications

Philanthropy and charitable organizations

Philanthropy and charitable organizations play a vital role in addressing social challenges and making a positive impact on society. However, traditional philanthropic systems often face issues of transparency, accountability, and inefficiency. Blockchain technology offers a transformative solution by providing a decentralized, transparent, and secure platform for philanthropic initiatives. This section explores the potential of blockchain in revolutionizing philanthropy and charitable organizations, examining the benefits, challenges, and applications of this integration, and discussing the implications for social impact and global giving.

Philanthropy encompasses the act of giving time, resources, or expertise to promote the welfare of others. Charitable organizations, including non-profit entities, foundations, and NGOs, facilitate the distribution of resources and drive social change in areas such as education, healthcare, poverty alleviation, and environmental conservation. Traditional philanthropic systems often face issues such as lack of transparency, limited donor engagement, high administrative costs, and inefficiencies in fund distribution. These challenges can impede the effectiveness and impact of charitable initiatives.

Blockchain's transparent and immutable nature provides a verifiable record of transactions and fund flows, ensuring transparency and accountability in philanthropic activities. Donors can track their contributions, and stakeholders can access real-time information about fund utilization, ensuring trust and fostering greater donor confidence.

Smart contracts, self-executing agreements kept on the blockchain, enable automated and efficient philanthropic operations. These contracts can facilitate transparent distribution of funds, automate verification of project milestones, and ensure that funds are allocated only to predefined purposes, reducing administrative costs and enhancing efficiency.

Blockchain enables direct peer-to-peer transactions, eliminating intermediaries and fostering direct engagement between donors and beneficiaries. This disintermediation facilitates personalized interactions, enables micro-donations, and builds stronger relationships between donors and charitable organizations.

Blockchain enables transparent tracking of fund distribution, ensuring that donations reach intended beneficiaries and reducing the risk of misappropriation. This transparency enhances trust, increases donor confidence, and encourages more individuals to contribute to charitable causes.

Blockchain can facilitate seamless and cost-effective cross-border donations by taking away the need for middlemen and reducing transaction fees. Cryptocurrencies and digital wallets powered by blockchain technology enable secure and immediate transfers, enabling faster aid disbursement to disaster-stricken areas or regions in need.

Blockchain allows for the tokenization of assets, enabling fractional ownership and liquidity. Donors can tokenize their assets, such as real estate or artwork, and contribute them to charitable organizations. These assets can be easily traded, providing a sustainable source of funding for philanthropic initiatives.

The widespread adoption and integration of blockchain in the philanthropic sector require collaboration among charitable organizations, donors, regulators, and technology providers. Education and awareness campaigns are crucial to promote the benefits of blockchain, address concerns, and encourage stakeholders to embrace this transformative technology.

While blockchain provides transparency, ensuring data privacy and security is paramount. Personal information of beneficiaries and donors must be protected, and privacy-preserving techniques, such as zero-knowledge proofs or private blockchains, should be explored to strike the right balance between transparency and privacy.

Blockchain scalability remains a challenge, particularly when dealing with large-scale philanthropic initiatives. Innovations such as Layer 2 solutions, off-chain processing, and interoperability protocols need to be developed to address scalability concerns and ensure the smooth functioning of blockchain-based philanthropic systems.

By leveraging blockchain, philanthropic organizations can enhance trust and accountability in the sector. Donors will have increased confidence that their contributions are utilized effectively, encouraging more individuals to participate in philanthropic activities.

Blockchain enables direct peer-to-peer transactions, allowing donors to have a direct impact on beneficiaries. This inclusivity empowers individuals, bypasses traditional intermediaries, and facilitates support for marginalized communities and grassroots initiatives.

Blockchain-based smart contracts streamline administrative processes, reducing costs and enabling more efficient allocation of resources. This ensures that a higher percentage of donations directly contribute to impactful projects, maximizing the social impact of philanthropic efforts.

Blockchain technology holds immense potential for revolutionizing philanthropy and charitable organizations. By leveraging its decentralized, transparent, and secure nature, blockchain can address the challenges faced by traditional philanthropic systems, ensuring transparency, accountability, and efficiency in fund distribution. However, addressing challenges related to adoption, privacy, and scalability is crucial to realizing the full potential of blockchain in philanthropy. Through collaboration, education, and responsible implementation, blockchain-powered philanthropy has the power to drive social impact, foster global giving, and create a more equitable and sustainable future.

Voting and governance systems

Voting and governance systems are at the core of democratic societies, enabling citizens to participate in decision-making processes and ensuring the fair representation of their interests. However, traditional voting systems often face challenges related to transparency, security, and trust. Blockchain technology has appeared as a potential solution, offering decentralized, transparent, and immutable platforms for voting and governance. This section explores the potential of blockchain in transforming voting and governance systems, examining the benefits, challenges, and applications of this integration, and discussing the implications for strengthening democracy and ensuring transparency.

Voting enables citizens to exercise their democratic rights, participate in the decision-making process, and hold their elected representatives accountable. It is a fundamental pillar of democracy and a means for individuals to shape the future of their society. Governance systems encompass the structures and processes that define how decisions are made and how power is exercised within a society. This includes both political governance (e.g., elections, legislation) and corporate governance (e.g., shareholder voting, board decisions).

Traditional voting systems often lack transparency, making it difficult to verify the integrity of the process. This can lead to doubts about the fairness of elections and decisions, eroding public trust in the system. Traditional voting systems are susceptible to security vulnerabilities, such as tampering, hacking, or fraud. These vulnerabilities can compromise the integrity and accuracy of the voting process, undermining the legitimacy of the outcomes. Traditional voting systems may face challenges related to accessibility, preventing certain groups from fully participating in the democratic process. This can lead to underrepresentation and inequalities in decision-making.

Blockchain's transparent and immutable nature enables the creation of tamper-proof voting and governance systems. Every transaction and decision recorded on the blockchain can be verified and audited, ensuring transparency and boosting public trust. Blockchain's cryptographic protocols and decentralized architecture provide robust security measures against tampering and fraud. The distributed nature of the blockchain ensures that data cannot be easily altered, enhancing the integrity of the voting and governance processes. Blockchain eliminates the need for a central authority in voting and governance systems. The consensus mechanisms employed in blockchain ensure that decisions are made collectively, fostering trust among participants and reducing the potential for corruption.

Blockchain can enable secure and transparent elections by recording votes on an immutable ledger. Each vote is cryptographically sealed and verifiable, ensuring that only eligible voters can participate and preventing tampering or manipulation of the results. Blockchain can facilitate decentralized governance systems, where decisions are made collectively by stakeholders. Smart contracts can automate decision-making processes, ensuring that actions are executed as per predefined rules and enhancing the efficiency of governance systems. Blockchain can streamline shareholder voting in corporate governance, enabling transparent and efficient voting processes. Shareholders can securely cast their votes and have their ownership rights accurately recorded on the blockchain, promoting shareholder engagement and ensuring fair decision-making.

The widespread adoption of blockchain-based voting and governance systems requires education, infrastructure development, and overcoming resistance to change. Ensuring accessibility for all individuals, including those with limited technological access or digital literacy, is crucial to avoid exacerbating inequalities. Preserving privacy while ensuring the transparency and auditability of voting and governance systems is a challenge. Techniques such as zero-knowledge proofs or privacy-preserving algorithms need to be explored to strike the right balance between data protection and transparency. Blockchain scalability remains a challenge when it comes to handling large-scale voting processes. Innovative solutions, such as Layer 2 protocols or off-chain processing, need to be developed to ensure the efficiency and scalability of blockchain-based voting and governance systems.

Blockchain-based voting systems can increase voter confidence by providing transparent and secure mechanisms. This, in turn, encourages broader participation, ensuring a more representative and inclusive democratic process. The use of blockchain in governance systems fosters trust by ensuring transparency, accountability, and integrity. Citizens can have greater trust in the decision-making processes, leading to more effective governance and improved public perception of institutions. Blockchain-based voting and governance systems have the potential for global applications, enabling secure and transparent elections in regions with weak democratic infrastructure or prone to corruption. This can contribute to democratization efforts worldwide.

Blockchain technology has the capacity to revolutionize voting and governance systems, addressing the challenges faced by traditional approaches. By leveraging its transparency, security, and decentralization, blockchain can enhance trust, strengthen democracy, and ensure transparency in decision-making processes. However, adoption, privacy, and scalability remain critical considerations in realizing the full potential of blockchain-based voting and governance systems. With careful implementation, collaboration, and responsible innovation, blockchain can contribute to a more inclusive, participatory, and transparent democratic landscape.

Refugee identification and aid distribution

One of the most urgent humanitarian issues of our day is the ongoing global refugee crisis. Due to violence, persecution, and natural disasters, millions of people have been compelled to escape their homes in search of safety as well as security in other countries. However, managing and delivering aid to refugees often faces significant challenges related to identification, verification, and the distribution of resources. In recent years, blockchain technology has appeared as a promising solution to enhance the efficiency, security, and transparency of refugee identification and aid distribution. This section explores the potential of blockchain in transforming the refugee assistance ecosystem, examining the benefits, challenges, and applications of this integration, and discussing the implications for empowering refugees and improving humanitarian response.

The global refugee crisis encompasses millions of displaced individuals seeking refuge across borders. The United Nations High Commissioner for Refugees (UNHCR) estimates that the quantity of forcibly displaced persons has exceeded 80 million, with over 26 million classified as refugees. The challenges faced in providing assistance to refugees include inadequate identification systems, lack of trust and transparency, limited access to financial services, and inefficiencies in aid distribution. These challenges hinder the provision of timely and targeted support to those in need.

Blockchain technology offers several benefits for refugee identification. Firstly, it provides secure and immutable identity records. By storing identity information on the blockchain, refugees can have a verifiable and tamper-proof digital identity, ensuring accurate identification and reducing the risk of identity fraud. Secondly, blockchain-based identification systems enable refugees to access essential services such as education, healthcare, and financial services. Digital identities on the blockchain can be used as a basis for providing secure and efficient access to these services, empowering refugees and promoting their integration into host communities. Lastly, blockchain allows refugees to have greater control over their personal data. Through self-sovereign identity solutions, refugees can selectively share their information with trusted entities, maintaining their privacy while participating in essential activities and aid programs.

Blockchain technology can revolutionize aid distribution processes for refugees. By leveraging its transparency and immutability, aid transactions can be tracked and audited on the blockchain. This reduces the risk of corruption, misappropriation, and inefficiencies in aid distribution. Smart contracts, which are self-executing agreements stored on the blockchain, can automate and streamline aid distribution processes. They ensure that aid reaches intended beneficiaries in a timely and targeted manner, reducing bureaucracy and administrative costs. Additionally, blockchain enables the secure and efficient transfer of digital currencies, facilitating direct cash transfers to refugees. Digital wallets powered by blockchain technology allow refugees to receive funds directly, eliminating the need for intermediaries and lessening the risk of funds being diverted or misused.

Implementing blockchain solutions for refugee identification and aid distribution comes with its own set of challenges. The digital divide presents a significant hurdle, as equitable access to technology, connectivity, and digital literacy is crucial to avoid excluding vulnerable populations from the benefits of blockchain-based systems. Interoperability and standardization are also essential for the effective implementation of blockchain in refugee assistance. Collaboration between organizations, governments, and technology providers is necessary to establish common protocols and ensure compatibility between different blockchain systems. Data protection as well as privacy are of utmost importance as sensitive personal data is stored on the blockchain. Robust encryption techniques, privacy-preserving algorithms, and legal frameworks should be in place to safeguard the confidentiality and integrity of refugee information.

The integration of blockchain in refugee identification and aid distribution holds significant implications for empowering refugees and improving humanitarian response. Firstly, it enhances refugee agency by providing them with secure digital identities and control over their personal data. This enables them to actively participate in decision-making processes, access services, and contribute to their own well-being. Secondly, blockchain technology improves accountability and transparency in refugee assistance programs. Donors, aid organizations, and host governments can track the flow of resources, ensuring that aid reaches its intended recipients and promoting transparency in humanitarian response. Lastly, blockchain facilitates trust and collaboration among different stakeholders involved in refugee assistance, including governments, NGOs, and international organizations. The transparent and secure nature of blockchain enhances coordination efforts, fostering more effective and efficient humanitarian response.

Blockchain technology has the potential to transform refugee identification and aid distribution, addressing the challenges faced by traditional systems. By leveraging its attributes of transparency, security, and efficiency, blockchain can enhance the accuracy of refugee identification, streamline aid distribution processes, and empower refugees in their journey towards self-reliance and integration. However, the adoption and implementation of blockchain solutions for refugees require collaboration, investment in technological infrastructure, and a commitment to ensuring inclusivity and privacy protection. With careful consideration of the challenges and responsible deployment, blockchain can contribute to improving the lives of refugees, strengthening humanitarian response, and fostering a more inclusive and resilient global society.

Impact on developing economies

Blockchain technology has appeared as a disruptive force with the potential to transform industries and traditional systems. While much of the discourse around blockchain focuses on its impact on developed economies, it is equally important to explore its implications for developing economies. These economies face unique challenges, including limited access to financial services, inadequate infrastructure, and bureaucratic inefficiencies. This section aims to examine the impact of blockchain technology on developing economies, analyzing its potential to drive inclusive growth, foster financial inclusion, promote transparency, and address key challenges. By understanding the opportunities and considerations that arise in developing economies, policymakers and stakeholders can harness the transformative power of blockchain to unlock economic potential and advance social development.

Developing economies are marked by diverse challenges, including limited access to financial services, high levels of poverty, inadequate infrastructure, and bureaucratic inefficiencies. These challenges, while significant, also present opportunities for blockchain technology to address key socio-economic issues. Economic development is critical for improving living standards, reducing poverty, and promoting social progress in developing economies. Blockchain technology has the ability to drive economic development by providing innovative solutions to existing challenges.

One of the fundamental challenges in developing economies is limited access to financial services. Blockchain technology can help overcome this barrier by providing decentralized and inclusive financial systems. Through blockchain-based platforms, individuals can securely store and transfer funds, access credit, and participate in the digital economy.

Remittances play a vital role in developing economies, contributing to poverty reduction and economic stability. Blockchain-powered remittance platforms can streamline and reduce the cost of cross-border transactions, benefiting both individuals and businesses. By eliminating intermediaries and reducing transaction fees, blockchain facilitates faster and more affordable remittances, supporting economic growth and poverty reduction.

Developing economies often face significant challenges related to corruption, lack of transparency, and weak governance structures. Blockchain's transparent and immutable nature can help address these challenges by providing a verifiable record of transactions, reducing corruption risks, and enhancing accountability. Supply chain transparency is crucial for developing economies, particularly in industries including agriculture and manufacturing. Blockchain can improve supply chain transparency by tracking and verifying the movement of goods from producers to consumers. This enables greater trust, reduces fraud, and ensures fair compensation for small-scale producers, thereby strengthening local economies.

Identity management is a key challenge in developing economies, as a significant portion of the population lacks formal identification. Blockchain-based identity management systems can provide individuals with secure and portable digital identities, enabling access to services such as education, healthcare, and social welfare. This empowers individuals and reduces the barriers they face in social and economic participation.

Land tenure issues are prevalent in developing economies, often leading to disputes and conflicts. Blockchain can address these challenges by providing secure and tamper-proof land registries. Through blockchain-based systems, individuals can establish and prove their land ownership, facilitating investment, economic growth, and poverty reduction.

The successful implementation of blockchain technology in developing economies requires adequate infrastructure and connectivity. Efforts must be made to improve internet access, digital literacy, and technological capabilities to ensure widespread adoption and maximize the benefits of blockchain. Developing economies must develop appropriate regulatory frameworks that balance innovation and consumer protection. Governments need to proactively engage with blockchain technology, fostering an enabling environment that encourages investment and innovation while addressing potential risks. Building the necessary skills and capacity to develop, deploy, and maintain blockchain solutions is crucial for the sustainable adoption of the technology in developing economies. Training programs and initiatives should be implemented to enhance technical expertise and promote entrepreneurship in the blockchain sector.

Blockchain technology can stimulate economic activity, entrepreneurship, and job creation in developing economies. By reducing barriers to entry, enabling secure transactions, and fostering trust, blockchain empowers individuals and communities, driving inclusive growth. The acceptance of blockchain technology can improve the stability, efficiency, and transparency of financial systems in developing economies. This, in turn, can attract investment, facilitate access to credit, and promote responsible financial practices, fostering economic resilience. Blockchain technology aligns with several Sustainable Development Goals (SDGs), including reducing poverty, promoting gender equality, enhancing financial inclusion, and ensuring sustainable economic growth. Its integration into development strategies can accelerate progress towards achieving these goals.

Blockchain technology holds immense potential for transforming developing economies by driving inclusive growth, fostering financial inclusion, promoting transparency, and addressing key challenges. By leveraging blockchain's unique features, developing economies can overcome existing barriers, create new economic opportunities, and improve the lives of their citizens. However, realizing the full potential of blockchain requires addressing infrastructure gaps, developing appropriate regulatory frameworks, and building the necessary skills and capacity. With strategic planning, collaboration, and responsible deployment, blockchain can become a catalyst for sustainable development, empowering individuals and propelling developing economies towards a prosperous future.

CONCLUSION

Recap of key insights and takeaways

Throughout this e-book, we have explored the transformative potential of blockchain technology across various sectors and applications. From healthcare to governance systems, financial services to supply chain management, blockchain has emerged as a disruptive force that promises transparency, security, and efficiency. In this final section, we recap the key insights and takeaways from our exploration, highlighting the overarching themes and implications of blockchain adoption. By revisiting these insights, we can better understand the immense possibilities that blockchain offers and pave the way for a transformed future.

Blockchain's Impact on Industries:

Blockchain technology has the capacity to revolutionize industries by introducing decentralized, transparent, and immutable systems. Across sectors such as finance, supply chain, healthcare, and governance, blockchain offers benefits such as enhanced security, streamlined processes, reduced costs, and increased trust. The key takeaway is that blockchain has the power to reshape traditional systems, remove intermediaries, and foster a new era of efficiency and collaboration.

Advantages of Blockchain:

Blockchain's inherent transparency enables stakeholders to access an immutable record of transactions and activities. This promotes trust among participants, reduces the need for intermediaries, and enables greater accountability. Blockchain's cryptographic algorithms and decentralized structure make it highly secure against tampering and fraud. The immutability of blockchain data ensures the integrity of information, providing a reliable source of truth. By removing intermediaries, automating processes through smart contracts, and streamlining data sharing, blockchain technology offers significant efficiency gains. These improvements lead to cost reduction, faster transaction settlements, and enhanced operational efficiency.

Challenges and Considerations:

Despite its promising potential, blockchain adoption faces several challenges that need to be addressed for widespread implementation:

As blockchain networks grow, scalability becomes a concern. Efforts are needed to develop solutions that can handle large transaction volumes without compromising speed, energy consumption, or decentralization. Blockchain operates across borders and challenges traditional regulatory frameworks. Governments and policymakers need to develop suitable regulations that strike a balance between innovation as well as consumer protection. While blockchain offers transparency, there are concerns regarding privacy and data protection. Striking the right balance between transparency and individual privacy is crucial, and technologies like zero-knowledge proofs can be employed to preserve confidentiality.

Collaboration and Interoperability:

To unlock the full potential of blockchain, collaboration and interoperability between different blockchain networks and platforms are essential. Standards and protocols need to be established to enable seamless communication and data sharing, fostering a network effect that amplifies the benefits of blockchain technology.

Ethical Considerations:

Blockchain technology raises ethical questions related to data ownership, governance, and inclusion. It is important to ensure that blockchain solutions are developed and implemented in a manner that respects individual rights, promotes inclusivity, and addresses biases and discrimination.

Empowering Individuals and Communities:
Blockchain has the potential to empower individuals as well as communities by giving them greater control over their data, enabling financial inclusion, and fostering trust. Through self-sovereign identity, decentralized finance, and peer-to-peer systems, blockchain can provide opportunities for economic empowerment and social development.

Driving Innovation and Transformation:
Blockchain is not a one-size-fits-all solution but rather a foundation for innovation and transformation. By encouraging research, development, and experimentation, we can uncover new use cases and disruptive applications that can reshape industries and societies.

Blockchain technology holds tremendous potential to transform industries, revolutionize traditional systems, and empower individuals. Through transparency, security, and efficiency, blockchain can address key challenges across sectors and unlock new opportunities for economic and social development. However, realizing the full potential of blockchain requires collaboration, addressing scalability and regulatory challenges, and fostering an ethical and inclusive approach. By embracing these insights and takeaways, we can harness the power of blockchain for a transformed future, where trust, transparency, and collaboration become the pillars of our digital society.

Anticipated future developments and adoption

Blockchain technology has witnessed rapid growth and adoption in recent years, revolutionizing various industries and challenging traditional systems. As we look to the future, it is crucial to explore the anticipated developments and adoption trends that will shape the trajectory of blockchain technology. In this section, we delve into the potential future developments of blockchain, examining emerging trends, challenges, and opportunities. By understanding the evolving landscape of blockchain adoption, we can prepare for a future where blockchain becomes an integral part of our digital infrastructure.

Evolution of Blockchain Technology:

From Cryptocurrencies to Diverse Applications:

Blockchain technology initially gained prominence through cryptocurrencies like Bitcoin. However, its potential extends far beyond financial transactions. We anticipate that blockchain will find applications in areas such as supply chain management, healthcare, energy, governance, and beyond, as organizations recognize its benefits in enhancing transparency, security, and efficiency.

Interoperability and Collaboration:

As blockchain adoption continues to grow, the need for interoperability and collaboration between different blockchain networks will become more pronounced. Standards and protocols will require to be developed to enable seamless data exchange, interoperability, and cross-chain transactions.

Anticipated Future Developments:

Scalability Solutions:

Scalability remains a crucial challenge for widespread blockchain adoption. To address this, various solutions are being explored, including layer 2 solutions like payment channels and sidechains, sharding techniques, and advancements in consensus mechanisms. These developments will enhance transaction throughput and enable blockchain networks to handle large-scale applications.

Privacy and Confidentiality Enhancements:

Privacy concerns have been a topic of discussion in the blockchain community. Anticipated developments include the integration of privacy-enhancing technologies like zero-knowledge proofs, homomorphic encryption, and secure multi-party computation. These innovations will enable individuals and organizations to maintain confidentiality while leveraging the benefits of blockchain technology.

Integration with Emerging Technologies:

Blockchain technology is likely to integrate with other emerging technologies to unlock new possibilities. Integration with artificial intelligence (AI) and machine learning (ML) will enhance smart contract capabilities and enable more sophisticated data analysis. Internet of Things (IoT) devices will be connected to blockchain networks, enabling secure and decentralized communication and data exchange.

Energy-Efficient and Sustainable Solutions:

The environmental impact of blockchain, particularly proof-of-work consensus mechanisms, has been a subject of concern. Future developments will focus on energy-efficient consensus mechanisms, such as proof-of-stake and proof-of-authority, and exploring the use of renewable energy sources for blockchain operations. These developments will align blockchain technology with sustainable and environmentally friendly practices.

Adoption Trends and Challenges:

Enterprise Adoption:

We anticipate increased adoption of blockchain technology by enterprises across various sectors. Organizations will recognize the value of blockchain in enhancing supply chain transparency, data security, and trust among stakeholders. Collaborative efforts between industry players, government agencies, and technology providers will drive enterprise adoption.

Government and Regulatory Frameworks:

Governments around the world are exploring blockchain adoption and the development of regulatory frameworks. These frameworks will address concerns such as consumer protection, data privacy, and legal recognition of blockchain-based transactions. Regulatory clarity will provide a conducive environment for blockchain innovation and adoption.

Education and Talent Development:

As blockchain technology expands its footprint, the need for skilled professionals will rise. Educational institutions and training programs will be vital in equipping individuals with the knowledge as well as skills required to develop, implement, and manage blockchain solutions. Investment in talent development will be crucial for successful blockchain adoption.

Opportunities and Implications:

Democratization of Access:

Blockchain technology has the capacity to democratize access to financial services, information, and opportunities. It can empower individuals in underserved regions, enabling financial inclusion, secure digital identities, and access to global markets. Blockchain's decentralized nature removes intermediaries, enabling direct peer-to-peer transactions and reducing barriers to entry.

Economic Growth and Innovation:

Blockchain technology has the capacity to drive economic growth by fostering innovation and entrepreneurship. It enables new business models, streamlines processes, and reduces costs. The adoption of blockchain by startups and established enterprises alike will create new job opportunities and stimulate economic development.

Trust and Transparency:

Blockchain's transparent and immutable nature enhances trust among stakeholders. It enables auditable and verifiable records, reducing the risk of fraud, corruption, and manipulation. This trust and transparency will lead to improved efficiency, better governance, and enhanced collaboration among individuals, organizations, and governments.

As we anticipate future developments and adoption of blockchain technology, we can envision a world where decentralized, transparent, and efficient systems become the norm. Scalability solutions, privacy enhancements, integration with emerging technologies, and sustainable practices will drive blockchain's evolution. Enterprise adoption, regulatory frameworks, and talent development will shape the landscape of blockchain adoption. The opportunities are vast, ranging from financial inclusion to economic growth and trust-building. By embracing these anticipated developments, we can unlock the full potential of blockchain technology and build a future that is secure, transparent, and empowered by decentralized systems.

Encouraging readers to explore and engage with blockchain technology

Blockchain technology has appeared as a transformative force, reshaping industries and revolutionizing traditional systems. As readers conclude this e-book, it is essential to motivate and empower them to explore and engage with blockchain technology. By actively participating in the blockchain ecosystem, readers can unlock new horizons of innovation, contribute to the development of the technology, and shape its future trajectory. In this section, we discuss the importance of embracing blockchain, provide guidance on how to get involved, and highlight the potential benefits of active engagement. By encouraging readers to explore and engage with blockchain, we can collectively harness its power to drive positive change.

Understanding the Importance of Blockchain Engagement:

Blockchain's Ubiquitous Potential:

Blockchain technology has the potential to impact diverse sectors, ranging from supply chain management and to healthcare and governance. By engaging with blockchain, readers can actively contribute to solving real-world challenges and drive innovation across industries.

Empowering Individuals and Communities:

Blockchain empowers individuals by giving them control over their data, enhancing financial inclusion, and promoting transparent governance. Engagement with blockchain allows readers to shape their digital identities, participate in decentralized finance, and contribute to the development of governance systems built on trust and transparency.

Ways to Explore and Engage with Blockchain:

Educate Yourself:

Begin by expanding your knowledge and understanding of blockchain technology. Explore online resources, attend webinars and workshops, and enroll in blockchain-related courses. By enhancing your understanding, you can navigate the blockchain ecosystem more effectively.

Join Blockchain Communities:

Engage with like-minded individuals and experts in blockchain communities. Participate in discussion groups, forums, and social media platforms dedicated to blockchain technology. Collaborate, ask questions, and share ideas to gain insights and expand your network.

Experiment with Blockchain Applications:

Start experimenting with blockchain applications and decentralized platforms. Set up a cryptocurrency wallet, participate in decentralized finance (DeFi) protocols, and explore blockchain-based applications and smart contracts. Hands-on experience will deepen your understanding and help you identify potential use cases.

Benefits of Active Engagement:

Professional Opportunities:

Blockchain expertise is in high demand across various industries. Active engagement with blockchain technology can open up new career pathways, entrepreneurial opportunities, and consulting roles. By staying abreast of the latest developments, readers can position themselves as leaders in this burgeoning field.

Innovative Solutions:

Active engagement with blockchain enables readers to identify gaps and challenges in existing systems and develop innovative solutions. By leveraging blockchain's transparency, security, and efficiency, readers can contribute to building transformative applications that address real-world problems.

Contributing to Decentralization and Democratization:

Blockchain technology promotes decentralization and democratization. By actively participating in blockchain networks, readers can contribute to the decentralization of power and decision-making processes. Their involvement can lead to more inclusive systems that empower individuals and communities.

Overcoming Challenges and Building Trust:

Addressing Technical Challenges:

Blockchain technology is evolving rapidly, and there may be technical hurdles along the way. Overcoming these challenges requires perseverance, continuous learning, and collaboration with the broader blockchain community. By embracing challenges, readers can contribute to the improvement and maturation of blockchain technology.

Promoting Ethical and Responsible Use:

Engagement with blockchain necessitates an ethical and responsible approach. Readers should consider the social impact of blockchain applications, address concerns related to privacy and data protection, and actively promote inclusivity and diversity within the blockchain ecosystem.

As readers conclude this e-book, it is crucial to recognize the transformative power of blockchain technology and the opportunities it presents. By encouraging exploration and active engagement, we can unlock the full capacity of blockchain and drive positive change. Through education, collaboration, experimentation, and a commitment to ethical practices, readers can contribute to building a decentralized and inclusive future. Embracing blockchain technology is not only a personal endeavor but also a collective effort to shape the future of innovation, transparency, and trust. Let us all embark on this journey and explore the boundless possibilities that blockchain offers.

Thank you for buying and reading/listening to our book.
If you found this book useful/helpful please take a few minutes and
leave a review on the platform where you purchased our book.
Your feedback matters greatly to us.

www.ingramcontent.com/pod-product-compliance
Lightning Source LLC
Chambersburg PA
CBHW060927140726
47996CB00001B/408